S0-ATJ-614

The Secret of Paul the Apostle

The Secret of
Paul the Apostle

Joseph A. Grassi

ORBIS BOOKS
Maryknoll, New York 10545

Second Printing, October, 1980

The Catholic Foreign Mission Society of America (Maryknoll) recruits and trains people for overseas missionary service. Through Orbis Books Maryknoll aims to foster the international dialogue which is essential to mission. The books published, however, reflect the opinions of their authors and are not meant to represent the official position of the Society.

Scripture texts used in this work are taken from the NEW AMERICAN BIBLE, Copyright © 1970 by the Confraternity of Christian Doctrine, Washington, D.C., and used by permission of the copyright owner. All rights reserved.

Copyright © 1978 Orbis Books, Maryknoll, NY 10545

All rights reserved

Printed in the United States of America

Library of Congress Cataloging in Publication Data

Grassi, Joseph A.
   The secret of Paul the Apostle.

   1. Paul, Saint, Apostle. 2. Christian saints
—Turkey—Tarsus—Biography. 3. Tarsus, Turkey—
Biography. 4. Missions—History—Early church,
ca. 30-600. I. Title.
BS2506.G693   225.9'2'4   [B]   77-29045
ISBN 0-88344-454-2

225.924
P281
G76

L.I.F.E. College Library
1100 Glendale Blvd.
Los Angeles, Calif. 90026

Contents

029757

Introduction

In 1965, I wrote a book about Paul entitled *A World to Win: The Missionary Methods of Paul the Apostle.* At that time I expressed my purpose as follows: "Many hundreds of books have been written on St. Paul. Few, however, have dealt with him precisely in his specific call to be an apostle, a man sent to establish new foundations where little or nothing had been done." Since that time, I have continued to remain a student of Paul, though I have wavered at times. I have become more and more convinced that he is, in the words of Augustine, "The Man Who Knew Christ Best." This book has been so considerably changed, improved, and rewritten that it cannot be claimed to be a revised edition of that first book.

When I wrote in 1965, I directed the book's message and applications especially to Christian missionaries. Now the audience still includes them, but is much broader as well: It includes any Christian who is deeply concerned to recover or deepen the essential apostolic element in the Christian message. By this I mean the basic impetus within Christianity that prompts us to share that faith with others by example and words.

My emphasis will still be on the "method" of Paul. This is not the dictionary sense of the word: "a procedure or process for attaining an object." It is "method" in the original sense, that of a "following after." Accordingly I shall deal with the qualities of lifestyle that emerge from a study of Paul. I call the book *The Secret of Paul the Apostle,* because it deals with the new basic insights and dynamic energy within that made him the man most responsible for western Christianity as we know it.

In studying the Apostle, my first source of information will be his own letters. Within the Pauline collection there are some letters, especially Colossians, Ephesians, and 1 and 2 Timothy, about which questions of authenticity have been raised. However, regardless of these questions, these letters are definitely Pauline, at least in the sense of their source in circles close to Paul. I will use them when they go along with or build on the earlier, more certain letters of Paul. To a lesser extent I have used the Acts of the Apostles, conscious that we cannot always know how much Luke's theology and literary plan influenced his portrait of Paul.

At the end of each chapter I have added some suggestions for the modern Christian. I am sure that Paul himself would smile at them. He would be the last person on earth who would want anyone slavishly to imitate him. He would want you to experience the same, if not greater love of Christ that animated him, and to enjoy the greatest flexibility and freedom in bringing Christ to the world of today. So these applications remain tentative and limited, for Paul should be allowed to speak for himself to each person today. In addition, if Paul were alive today he would be the first to acknowledge his own limitations when it came to expressing the social message of the gospel. Paul's message was radical for his own time and continues to challenge the world of today. However, the Holy Spirit has been active for almost two thousand years since his time and continues to open up new and exciting dimensions for the application of the gospel.

1

His Conversion: Vision of a New World

Western Christianity has been made possible for the most part by the work of one man, Paul the Apostle. How can we account for the tremendous success of one fervent Jew in implanting so many churches throughout Europe and Asia Minor? What was the source of his boundless energy in traveling hundreds of miles on foot from city to city, always in extreme danger from robbers, bitter persecutors, and even his former friends? We would search in vain through his letters and the Acts of the Apostles for a list of techniques or methods that would account for his amazing achievements. The secret of his success is found first of all in the nature of his conversion experience while on the road to Damascus. This was the decisive turn in his life.

To understand the impact of his conversion to Christ, it is first essential to understand his former life in Judaism. He was born in Tarsus, in the Roman Province of Asia, which would be near the southern coast of modern Turkey. Jews outside of Palestine lived in closely knit communities in the same geographical sections of cities and villages in the Greek world. They did this so they could practice all the regulations of the Jewish Torah, or Law. This was not "law" in the modern sense of the word. It was a whole way of life that included religious observances, customs, ritual, and ethical regulations. It was essentially a way of continually remembering God and bringing his presence and power into all the events of daily life. It was really prayer in action. The Torah was commonly regarded as a "fence" which protected the Jews from infiltration and influence by the powerful forces of the Greek world that surrounded them. In addition it was a discipline in the sense that it trained men and women to order their lives in accord with the high ethical ideals found in the Bible. Many of the regulations of the Torah concerned food, especially the proper slaughtering of meat and preserving food from impurities and contact with Gentile hands. This meant that real fellowship with Gentiles was almost impossible, because this would usually entail meals together. It meant that Jews had to live together in an enclave where they could be assured the support and atmosphere necessary for keeping the Torah.

Paul's family atmosphere was deeply religious. He was raised in strict conformity with Jewish ideals. To make it possible for him to have the best available education, he was sent to Jerusalem as a child for further training (Acts 22:3). Here his training was essentially religious. In Jerusalem, the center of Judaism, he was able to learn from the best teachers of his time, including the well-known Gamaliel: "I was brought up in this city. Here I sat at the feet of Gamaliel and was educated strictly in the law of our fathers. I was a staunch defender of God" (Acts 22:3).

In addition to his strict Jewish upbringing, Paul also became a Pharisee. He always looked back on this, perhaps with a bit of secret pride: "I was circumcised on the eighth day, being of the stock of Israel and the tribe of Benjamin, a Hebrew of Hebrew origins; in legal observance I was a Pharisee" (Phil. 3:5). The Pharisees formed a select fervent group within Judaism. They were distinguished by an ardent zeal to bring the Torah into every detail of daily life. They also were noted for their earnest striving for absolute perfection in every detail of the Law. For example, the Torah (all the laws found in the Bible and in oral tradition) required a tithe donation to the Temple for every Jew. This was commonly interpreted as referring to wheat, oil, and wine. The Pharisees, however, gave a tenth of everything they had, even including garden herbs. In addition, the Pharisees took upon themselves not only all the biblical regulations for ordinary people; they also applied to themselves all the minute regulations that were only for priests. This was so they could preserve a very special holiness.

The Pharisees had their own religious meetings in addition to the synagogue and Temple. They usually met at least twice a month. To become a Pharisee was a matter of special initiation and long training. Special ascetical practices were learned and used in daily life, especially fasting. The Pharisees were regarded by the ordinary people as their religious leaders, teachers, and models. They were the ardent patriots of their time. They regarded the Romans and Greeks as intruders on their own religious and national freedom. There was to be no compromise between Greek culture and Judaism. The extension of the Law to all of daily life was meant to be a guarantee and protection of the Jewish faith.

The young man Paul plunged himself whole-heartedly into his Pharasaic training and soon became respected and noted as a prominent leader and teacher. Writing to the Philippians, he notes, "I was above reproach when it came to justice based on the law" (Phil. 3:6). To the Galatians he writes, "I made progress in Jewish observance far beyond most of my contemporaries, in the excess of zeal to live out all the traditions of my ancestors" (Gal. 1:14). Reading between the lines, we can sense some of the tremendous energy, discipline, and will power that went into such a life. There was also a deep sense of achievement that accompanied his efforts. He was looked up to as a model by many of his fellow Pharisees and Jews.

Great Expectations

As an ardent young Jew and Pharisee, he shared the common enthusiastic hopes and expectations for a coming dramatic intervention of God in human history. After all, the God of the Hebrews was a God of justice and peace who made ethical demands on his people and on the world. If he was a God of history, the world could not simply keep going along on its present path of separation, evil, and injustice. God simply *had* to intervene if he was God. This coming day of intervention had been foretold by many of the Hebrew prophets, who referred to it as "the Day of the Lord." This intervention in the world would overcome the barriers of separation between people and nations in order to make the world once again God's own one family. Jew and Gentile would once more be brought together.

Many Jews believed that this intervention would come to pass within human history and time. In other words, a transformation would take place here on earth among people in their own times and circumstances. However, there was also another very important stream of expectation. This we may call "apocalyptic." Apocalyptic means "unfolding," or "revealing." It refers to a secret plan of God, revealed to certain elect, that God will suddenly intervene in the world to bring an end to human history as we know it and open up an entirely new age and a new humanity. This type of hope was very evident during times of foreign domination, especially that of the Greeks and Romans, where conditions seemed so desperate and impossible that only a sweeping and cleansing intervention by God such as this could bring about the new promised age. Paul was very much moved by the apocalyptic movement. He saw his own fervent devotion to the Torah as the best possible means to speed the moment of God's great expected intervention in the world. Like most people he thought that this time was imminent and could happen in the very near future. When it did happen, the last days of present history would be at hand, and the new age would begin to open up.

What were some of the prominent characteristics of this great new age?

1. First of all, there would be cessation of war and the beginning of a new justice, peace, and harmony in the world. All the nations would join Israel once more and together be restored to God's one family.

> In the days to come, the mountain of the Lord's house shall be established as the highest mount and raised above the hills. All nations shall stream toward it; many peoples shall come and say "Come, let us climb the Lord's mountain, to the house of the God of Jacob, that he may instruct us in his ways, and we may walk in his paths." For from Zion shall go forth instruction, and the word of the Lord from Jerusalem. He shall judge between the nations, and impose terms on my peoples. They shall beat their swords into plowshares and their spears into pruning hooks; one nation shall not raise the sword against another, nor shall they train for war again [Isa. 2:2–4].

The above text is not referring simply to external peace, detente, or ceasefire. It is a matter of imitation of God and moral change. Specifically it is said that God will "instruct us in his ways, and we may walk in his paths." In addition, the word of God and his instruction will go out from Jerusalem and Zion.

2. The new age would be an age when all of God's power and Spirit would be evident in the world. In the Bible, the Spirit was the name given to God as manifest in the activity and life of people. It was first of all the source of all life, as when God breathed into the first human

being to give life (Gen. 2:7). But the Spirit was also the source of all that showed God's presence in people in quite an extraordinary or unusual way. The coming of the new age would be accompanied by the discovery of a new full dimension and depth of the Spirit of God that would result in exciting new manifestations of God's power and presence.

> Then afterward I will pour out my spirit upon all mankind. Your sons and daughters shall prophesy, your old men shall dream dreams, your young men shall see visions; even upon the servants and the handmaids, in those days, I will pour out my spirit. And I will work wonders in the heavens and on the earth [Joel 3:1–2].

Note the universality of this text: It refers to *all humankind.* Together the world will look to one God as their father and call out God's name in worship: "Then everyone shall be rescued who calls on the name of the Lord " (3:5).

3. The inner presence of the Spirit in the new age would bring about a great interior change and regeneration among men and women that would be evident in their lives. It would be a Spirit characterized by love, mercy, forgiveness, and reconciliation among people. It would be a new interior Torah written on people's hearts.

> This is the covenant which I will make with the house of Israel after those days, says the Lord. I will place my law within them, and write it upon their hearts; I will be their God, and they shall be my people. No longer will they have need to teach their friends and kinsmen how to know the Lord. All, from least to greatest, shall know me, says the Lord, for I will forgive their evil doing and remember their sin no more [Jer. 31:33–34].

> I will give them a new heart and put a new spirit
> within them; I will remove the stony heart from
> their bodies, and replace it with a natural heart,
> so that they will live according to my statutes,
> and observe and carry out my ordinances [Ezek.
> 11:19].

In Ezekiel, this cleansing action of the Spirit was likened
to the action of water as a symbol and sign of God's
presence:

> I will sprinkle clean water upon you to cleanse
> you from all your impurities, and from all your
> idols I will cleanse you. I will give you a new
> heart and place a new spirit within you, taking
> from your bodies your stony hearts and giving
> you natural hearts [Ezek. 36:26–27].

4. Most people believed that the new age would be
inaugurated through the action of an intermediary from
God, a messiah, or anointed one. Some thought of this
new era in earthly and national terms, and looked to a
restoration of the Davidic dynasty under a new leader.
This anointed one would free Israel from foreign domination and win respect for it among the nations of the
world. This group, however, although numbering many
zealous adherents, especially the revolutionary or Zealot
party, was in the minority. Paul and most of his friends
were more influenced by the abundant apocalyptic literature of the times that painted a brilliant picture of a
super-earthly kingdom to come into existence through
the powerful intervention of God. A mysterious "Son of
Man" figured largely in these writings; he would be
God's chosen instrument to inaugurate his kingdom on
the day when the divine power would burst upon the
earth from heaven.

5. Apocalyptic expectations included a great judgment
of God and the resurrection of the dead as a sure final

sign of the last days of the world. It would be a certain indication that the old world had ended and that the new age was beginning.

> Many of those who sleep in the dust of the earth shall awake; some shall live forever, others shall be an everlasting horror and disgrace [Dan. 12:2].

In the Gospel of John, we see some evidence of this popular belief. When Jesus tells Martha that her brother Lazarus will rise again, she replies, "I know that he will rise again in the resurrection on the last day" (John 11:23–24).

Jesus of Nazareth

The young Paul and Jesus were contemporaries. However, it is quite unlikely that they ever met. At least Paul makes no hint of it in his letters, and it would have been very advantageous to him if he could have appealed to a personal acquaintance with the earthly Jesus. There is no doubt, however, that he had heard about him. Everyone in Judea knew about the young prophet from Nazareth. He certainly knew about Jesus' essential proclamation that the kingdom of God was at hand here and now: that it was no longer a case of longing and looking for the future. Jesus had taught that the final countdown for the beginning of the new age was taking place at this moment in history. Paul knew that this Jesus had a reputation as a healer and teacher. He was most probably in Jerusalem itself at the time when Jesus was crucified by the Romans as a politically dangerous revolutionary messiah. Paul knew that it was the opposition of the chief priests and official Judaism that had prompted them to hand Jesus over to the Romans. As puppets of Rome, they were obliged to denounce to Rome any dangerous popular leaders. He knew that Jesus had challenged the Pharisees and religious leaders of the Jews by his own supreme independence and freedom. He was regarded as a threat to religious authority and national unity.

The news of the events that followed Jesus' death was indeed astonishing, as well as alarming. There was a small group of disciples of Jesus in the holy city and also elsewhere that believed that the crucified Jesus had risen from the dead and had appeared several times to their leaders, as well as to the assembled community. They believed that the Spirit of Jesus, which was the Spirit of God, was now present in them and working with extraordinary power. As a result, they were able to perform many signs and wonders, which included remarkable conversions as well as a continuation of the healing ministry of Jesus himself.

Paul with his deep insight into Judaism knew well the implications of what was going on. Jesus had claimed to be the last prophet of God, announcing his final intervention in the world. He was either a true prophet or a false prophet. Now that he was dead, the results had to be seen. Paul knew that the resurrection of a just man into God's glory and presence was considered an infallible sign of the last days of history, and that is what the followers of Jesus proclaimed. They announced that Jesus was truly the last prophet of the last times. God had raised him up from the dead by the mighty power of the Spirit to show them that all God's power had been working in Jesus and was now working *in them* to inaugurate the great new final age of God. This meant an entirely new perspective. If they were right, then Paul was following the ways of the old world which was coming to an end. If they were wrong, they could be dangerously misleading the people in a new direction that was entirely an illusion. It was an emphasis that might take their eyes off the supreme importance and centrality of the Torah.

At first it is hard to understand why Paul took upon himself an almost one-man campaign against the new sect. After all, messianic groups were nothing new. Many of his compatriots were rather favorably inclined toward members of the new sect, which had little to distinguish itself externally from their fellow Jews. But Paul saw beneath the surface, for he had listened carefully to the young Stephen as he made his defense before his martyrdom.

Stephen was one of the "seven" whom the twelve apostles had chosen to be their assistants. He was a Greek-speaking Jew and quickly proved to be one of the most brilliant lights in the young community. Luke makes it a point to draw special attention to the power of the Spirit that moved him. He was man "filled with grace and power" (Acts 6:8). His outspoken defense of the new faith soon brought about his arrest. The charges made against him were that he had spoken "against the Holy Place and the Law," that he had claimed that Jesus had said that he would "destroy this place [the Temple] and change the customs which Moses handed down to us" (Acts 6:13–14).

Although false witnesses had made these charges, there was a certain nucleus of truth behind them. Stephen was one of the first to see clearly that Jesus by his resurrection and the sending of his Spirit into his people had made a new living temple that took the place of the old material temple of the Jews. He also saw that the new faith would eventually supersede the regulations of the old law. He was not the type of man to keep these insights to himself and had openly expressed his views.

After his arrest, Stephen made his defense before the Sanhedrin. He forcibly pointed out that God's dwelling among his people was not limited or restricted by the Temple; he stated, "the Most High does not dwell in buildings made by human hands" (Acts 7:47). He accused them of restricting and opposing the Holy Spirit throughout the history of their people. At the end of his speech he looked up to heaven and saw Jesus standing at the right hand of God. The vision affirmed what he already knew, that the glory of God had entered into Jesus, who was now the Holy Temple of God. He told the Sanhedrin, "I see an opening in the sky, and the Son of Man standing at the right hand of God" (Acts 7:56). At this point they seized him, brought him outside the city, and stoned him to death. His enemies had been quick to see that Stephen's claim that Jesus himself was the Holy Temple of God would spell the end of worship in a material temple, and eventually nullify the cherished traditions of Moses.

Paul above all understood the deep meaning behind the words of Stephen. If his words were true, then God had inaugurated the final age of the world through this man Jesus. This went against everything he held most dear and sacred. As a good Jew, he held that the Torah was the revelation of God and the source of Israel's hope. He believed along with his fellow Pharisees that only a strict and zealous adherence to the Law would hasten the messianic age. If Stephen was right, then God had now completely shown himself in Jesus, independently of the Law; if this was so, then the Law could only become secondary and eventually lose its meaning for those who believed in Jesus.

Since Paul saw the implicit conflict between Judaism and the new "Way" so clearly there was nothing left for him to do but to devote all his energies to stamping out the believers in Jesus. Paul's whole life had been dedicated to bringing the blessings of the Law to as many people as possible in order to prepare the way for the final times. He had probably been a Jewish missionary before he became a Christian missionary. He wrote, "I made progress in Jewish observance far beyond most of my contemporaries in my expression of zeal to live out all the traditions of my ancestors" (Gal. 1:4). As a good Jew, he believed that missionary work was one of the principal means for hastening the coming of the messianic age. This was based on the teachings of the prophets who had predicted that the dawn of the great age would coincide with the conversion of the nations. Paul saw clearly that this new sect was nullifying all his life's work by implicitly undermining the position of the Law.

It is understandable then that he literally "went to extremes in persecuting the Church of God" (Gal. 1:13). It was imperative for him that the new group be suppressed as soon as possible. He was so convinced of this that it was not enough for him to seek out believers in Jerusalem; he even sought and obtained authority from the high priest to arrest members of the new sect in Damascus and bring them back in bonds to Jerusalem to face trial.

Vision of a New World

Little did Paul suspect that he would be the one to be brought back in bonds to Jerusalem. Jesus, the Son of God, captured him and Paul became his servant for life. Later Paul described this experience with the words, "I have been grasped by Christ Jesus" (Phil. 3:12). We might well ask what it was that could have made such a startling and sudden change in a man who had previously been such a violent persecutor of the church. First, let us look at his own brief testimony in his letters.

Paul describes his own vision of the risen Jesus in the same terms and on the same level as the original appearances of the Lord to Peter and the twelve.

> I handed on to you first of all what I myself received, that Christ died for our sins in accordance with the Scriptures; that he was buried, and, in accordance with the Scriptures, rose on the third day; that he was seen by Cephas, then

by the Twelve. After that he was seen by five
hundred brothers at once, most of whom are still
alive, although some have fallen asleep. Next he
was seen by James; then by all the apostles. Last
of all he was seen by me, as one born out of the
normal course. I am the least of the apostles; in
fact, I do not even deserve the name. But by
God's favor I am what I am [1 Cor. 15:3–9].

In this account, great significance is placed on the
fulfilment of Scriptures, which is twice mentioned. Paul
wants to emphasize that what has happened in the resurrection of Jesus is the completion of all of God's plan
working through history. He enumerates all the appari-
tions of the risen Jesus of which he has learned through a
living tradition that has come to him. His own apparition
is an additional confirmation that was given as a special
grace to him. The significance of the resurrection appari-
tions lies in the Jewish belief that one of the most certain
signs of the beginning of the final age of the world was to
be the resurrection of the just into God's glory. The
visions confirm that the last days of history, expected for
countless ages, are now at hand. Paul now knows
through his own personal experience that this is true.

In the biblical viewpoint, a person who is granted a
special apparition or vision of God does not regard it as
merely a personal privilege, but something that must be
shared with others. A divine communication constitutes
a person as a messenger of God, or prophet, who con-
veys God's words or action to the people. For this reason,
Paul felt he was called to be an apostle, one sent by God.
It was a special favor or grace granted for the benefit of
others. So he writes,

By God's favor I am what I am. This favor of his
to me has not proved fruitless. Indeed, I have
worked harder than all the others, not on my
own but through the favor of God. In any case,

whether it be I or they, this is what we preach and this is what you believed [1 Cor. 15:10–11].

The second reference of Paul to his conversion is a very brief one in 1 Cor. 9:1: "Have I not seen Jesus our Lord?" The use of the term "Lord" in reference to Jesus is very significant. In the Old Testament, "Lord" was a title given to God alone in view of his revelation to Israel and his power over all the universe. In Philippians, Paul writes of God's gift of his own name to Jesus:

> Because of this, God highly exalted him and bestowed on him the name above every other name, so that at Jesus' name every knee must bend in the heavens, on the earth and under the earth, and every tongue proclaim to the glory of God the Father: JESUS CHRIST IS LORD! [Phil: 2:9–11]

The title of Lord, then, emphasizes God's power as manifest in Jesus. God has initiated the last times of history by a mighty act of power in raising Jesus from the dead and sharing with him the title of Lord, master of the universe.

A third text is found in Galatians 1:15–16:

> But the time came when he who had set me apart before I was born and called me by his favor chose to reveal his Son to me, that I might spread among the Gentiles the good tidings concerning him.

Here again there is reference to the appointed, long-awaited time in history for the fulfilment of the divine plan. In his goodness, God had decided even before the birth of Paul to set him aside as a messenger of this good news. Three great themes are compressed in this short statement: revelation, sonship, and preaching to the Gentile world.

The verb "reveal" already points to the nature of his conversion. The Greek word for reveal or unfold is *apokalyptein*, which is very frequently linked with the final appearance, or *parousia*, of the Messiah, the Son of Man. We see such a link in Luke 17:30: "It will be like that on the day that the Son of Man is *revealed*." Likewise Paul writes to the Thessalonians about "when the Lord Jesus is revealed from heaven," on the great day of his appearance (2 Thess. 1:7). The words, then, would lead us to understand that Paul had a vision of the risen Son of Man coming in great triumph in the midst of his people. Or we should say, "beginning to come in triumph," for this "revelation" was only beginning to take place, and would come to pass completely only at the last day, for, as Paul writes in Romans, "The whole created world eagerly awaits the *revelation* of the sons of God" (Rom. 8:19).

The object of the revelation was the *Son* himself. The vision unfolded to Paul in some way who the Son was. It was not any external means or knowledge but by the presence of the risen Son himself through his Spirit. Joined to the risen Christ, through sharing his Spirit, Paul could know what it meant to be a son of God. He describes this very simply later on in the same epistle: "God sent forth his Son, born of a woman, . . . that we might receive our status as adopted sons. The proof that you are sons is the fact that God has sent forth into our hearts the Spirit of his Son which cries out, 'Abba, (Father)' " (Gal. 4:6).

Finally, the words "that I might spread among the Gentiles the good tidings" bring out some of the practical consequences of what had happened. If God had chosen Paul in such a striking manner, it was so he could be a living witness of God's intervention—that others could have the same hope and confidence of becoming true sons of God. Paul had received the Spirit that was in Jesus precisely that he might share him with others. Previously Paul had *something* to give people in the Law;

now he had *someone* to share—the Spirit of Jesus who in his great love wished to enter into countless men and women in order to form a permanent community of true brothers and sisters.

The specific mention of the Gentiles, the whole non-Jewish world, has special meaning. Paul knew well the Scriptures that had spoken of a day when all the nations of the world would rejoin Israel as the one family of God. He recognized that the great intervention of God in Jesus meant that God was inaugurating his final kingdom or rule on earth. Such news *must* be made known to the world, since the whole world would be affected by it. Even today, the inauguration of a new president or ruler calls for immediate notification to all the nations of the world. This is because all are affected in some way. Paul then felt the urgent need to bring the good news to the whole world. At the time of his conversion, like many others, he thought that it should go first to Israel and then to the world. As time went on, he learned from experience that he was to go directly to the Gentiles.

From the brief description in Galatians we can surmise that Paul's experience must have been very similar to that of Stephen as he died in martyrdom, looking up to heaven: "He saw the glory of God, and Jesus standing at God's right hand. 'Look!' he exclaimed, 'I see an opening in the sky, and the Son of Man standing at God's right hand' " (Acts 7:56).

A final text from Paul is found in 2 Cor. 4:6:

> God, who said, "Let light shine out of darkness," has shone in our hearts, that we in turn might make known the glory of God shining on the face of Christ.

This text is an indirect reflecting on his conversion experience. The emphasis is on God's light and glory. As Creator, God brought this light into existence by his mighty power. However, he brought the fulness of his light and presence into the world through Christ. Christ himself was transfigured with God's glory that shone through his whole person, especially his face. This same glory and light now shines in the heart of the believer, who becomes like Christ a light-filled, or luminous, being. In his conversion experience, Paul must have seen the divine light shining through Christ and shining through him in a community or body of believers joined to him.

In the Acts of the Apostles, we find a second-hand account of the conversion of Paul as related by Luke the evangelist:

> As he traveled along and was approaching Damascus, a light from the sky suddenly flashed about him. He fell to the ground and at the same time heard a voice saying, "Saul, Saul, why do you persecute me?" "Who are you, sir?" he asked. The voice answered, "I am Jesus, the one you are persecuting. Get up and go into the city, where you will be told what to do" [Acts 9:3–6].

This story adds the sudden realization by Paul that the Christian community, the very group he despised and so violently persecuted, was the dwelling place of Jesus the risen Messiah. When Paul asked, "Who are you?" the voice had responded, "I am Jesus, the one you are persecuting." Paul immediately understood the solidarity and identity of the risen Jesus with the new community. The risen Messiah was now mightily at work in his people. The conversion experience deeply impressed on Paul his own oneness with the Risen Jesus. It also taught him that the Christian community was a shining vessel through which Jesus' own Spirit manifested itself to the world. Later he would describe this presence in terms of what he would call the "Body of Christ." Another surprise to Paul was that the Messiah had come into the midst of very *ordinary* people. He had bypassed his own colleagues, the fervent Pharisees who were convinced that they were best preparing the way for the coming of the Messiah. The risen Jesus was also especially identified with suffering people: "I am Jesus, the one who you are persecuting." This was because they were so closely assimilated to the Master himself whose whole life centered about the cross.

To sum up: Paul the Pharisee had set out for Damascus to capture the followers of Jesus. Instead, Jesus captured him and Paul became his follower. Paul's conversion experience taught him that the final, long expected new age of the world had finally arrived. God had acted with all his power to raise Jesus from the dead and was now present and active through his Spirit in the Christian community. The community, through this Spirit, was a light-filled luminous body that reflected God's glory and presence to the world. Paul also understood that it was God's plan to reveal his Son to the world and create a permanent community of children of God united through fellowship with Christ. Paul's own special role was to be a participator in this plan and a witness to the world of what God was doing in him, and in others who had believed. Knowing that the risen Jesus had become Lord of the Universe, he was perfectly confident that God would act in him to faithfully accomplish his eternal design and plan.

Applications for Modern Christians

How do you look at yourself and the world that you live in? Do you really see things and people as they are, or according to an image in your mind that is very much influenced by the common view of people around you? The experience of Paul and others like him tells you that you must learn to look at the world with different eyes. And to do so, there must come first a certain blindness, like Paul's, to the world you commonly see. Once your eyes are opened again to a new, deeper dimension in all reality you will be surprised to find a whole new exciting view of the world and people around you:

1. You will become alert to an inner core or movement behind what seemed to be just ordinary haphazard events. You will see an inner movement, direction, and plan within human history. Since this movement has all the divine power behind it, you will find a new energy and direction in your own life as you surrender to this inner flow, rather than fighting against it in so many ways by merely relying on your own will power, achievement, or plans. Later Paul will call this surrender "faith." "Faith" means openness to what ordinarily seems beyond your capabilities and powers. It means openness to the impossible, at least according to human standards.

2. In place of the image of a cold, impersonal universe, you will find a warm, light-filled world that is friendly to you at its inner core. This is because it has an inner guidance and movement by the Spirit of God. Instead of ordinary, dull people, you will perceive luminous beings who have within them a divine spark ready to burst into open flame. You will become aware that every person you see has a birthright to the highest consciousness a human being can attain. This is the realization of the divine forces and personality working within them. Paul came to an understanding that the glory of God was shining in the Christian community through the presence of the Spirit of Christ. Yet he did not see others, in contrast, as being in darkness. In 2 Cor. 4:6, as we have seen, he saw the divine light and life as first brought to us by God in creation. The fulness of light through Christ was a second birth, a reawakening that brought out a fulness of divine light and life resulting from a seed already present.

3. Like Paul, you will see the world and people moving toward oneness and unity, according to the plan of God to bring back together his one human family. You will see the Spirit of God in all that moves to this oneness, and

cooperate actively in this wonderful inner movement. At the same time, you will take a definite stand against all that divides men and women or creates barriers between them due to race, sex, creed, culture, or education. For Paul, the one Christ was God's own instrument to create one community, one people, and eventually one world.

4. Once you have experienced the risen Christ, as Paul did, you will see this not as a private privilege or an individual matter. Paul saw this as a beautiful gift of grace that was at the same time a responsibility for him to share. The best way, then, for you to grow in realization of your gift is to share it with others. This does not mean "preaching at them" but just plain frankness and honesty with others about the things that are most deeply meaningful in your life. The Spirit within you is the contagious element that will move other people also to discover that same Spirit at work in their own lives. Words will always be secondary, but still important.

2

Identity with Christ

The great secret of Paul the Apostle was a very simple one: his deep inner experience of an intimate identity with Christ. He had a profound realization that the risen Jesus was working in him and through him. On the road to Damascus the Risen Lord had seized him; he became a man possessed by the powerful Spirit of the living and risen Jesus. The Spirit of the Master moved him to speak and to act with a power and confidence that was not his own. The tremendous love of Jesus for him became a dominant, impelling power in his life. From then on he felt that he really had someone to share with others. The gift of the Spirit of Jesus, which could be shared with others, was his greatest apologetic. The actual possession of the Spirit was to Paul a "proof," as we see from Galatians 3:2, where he writes: "How did you receive the Spirit? Was it through observance of the Law, or through faith in what you heard?"

As a result of his conviction that he was a witness to the risen Jesus, Paul did not need to appeal to outside proofs or point out examples from the past. It was enough for him to say, "Imitate me as I imitate Christ" (1 Cor. 11:1). As a result of this identification, he could write to the suffering community at Thessalonica, "You, in turn, become imitators of us and of the Lord . . . " (1 Thess. 1:6). For Paul, the glory of God had clearly shone on the face of Jesus. The effect of his conversion was the same glory shining through him by his union with Jesus. Reflecting on his own experience at Damascus where both his internal and external blindness had been cured by the light of Christ at Baptism, he wrote, "God who said, 'Let light shine out of darkness,' has shone in our hearts, that we might in turn make known the glory of God shining on the face of Christ" (2 Cor. 4:6). His encounter at Damascus was not a past event but a permanent experience.

This identification with Jesus was such a central part of his life that it formed a whole new principle of activity for him. As a result he could write to the Galatians,

> The life I live now is not my own; Christ is living in me. I still live my human life, but it is a life of faith in the Son of God, who loved me and gave himself for me [Gal. 2:20].

The "life of faith" he speaks of is a complete obedient surrender and openness to God's love as shown to him through and in Christ. This is why he speaks of "the Son of God, who loved me and gave himself for me."

This new life of faith was a complete reversal of his former life where he counted on discipline, will power, and achievement in order to obtain perfect observance of the Law. Surrender in faith now takes the place of achievement. Paul makes a very moving comparison to his previous life as he writes to the Philippians.

> Those things I used to consider gain I have now reappraised as loss in the light of Christ. I have come to rate all as loss in the light of the surpassing knowledge of my Lord Jesus Christ [Phil. 3:8].

The "knowledge" he speaks of is not intellectual but, according to the Hebrew meaning of "knowledge," a deep personal experience. Paul's one desire is "to know Christ and the power flowing from his resurrection"

(Phil. 3:10). This is so central to his life that even when faced with the prospect of death he has a difficult choice to make: "For, to me, 'life' means Christ; hence dying is so much gain. If, on the other hand, I am to go on living in the flesh, that means productive toil for me—and I do not know which to prefer" (Phil. 1:23).

Further dimensions of this identity with Christ may be discovered if we see how Paul describes the Christian baptismal experience, which was his own experience as well. To the Romans he writes, "Are you not aware that we who were baptized into Christ were baptized into his death" (Rom. 6:3). In ancient times, the adult was usually completely submerged in water. The word "baptism" means a "plunging into." Water itself symbolized both death and life. As the convert was plunged into the water, it was a symbolic death, or entering into the grave. Yet it was also a plunging into Christ in respect to the whole meaning of his life and death. This meaning was a radical separation or break from any sin or earthly power—a complete break from a former style of life in the world. The bodily action of baptism or submerging was actually a vow or promise made by the whole body-person to become exactly like Christ and be identified with him. With this new identity the candidate took on a new name, the very name of Christ himself. For this reason they were later called "Christians"—meaning people who belonged to Christ and bore his name.

The second part of this identification in baptism was a real union with Christ in his new risen life, a life completely dominated by the Spirit of God. This very Spirit of God had raised him from the dead precisely so he might share it with others: "Through baptism into his death we were buried with him, so that, just as Christ was raised from the dead by the glory of the Father, we too might live a new life" (Rom. 6:4). This new life is a duplication of the life of Jesus himself, since Jesus was completely led by the Spirit of God.

Paul then sees that identity with Christ has come

through sharing the same Spirit of God that was and is in Christ Jesus. As a result, Paul proclaims the astonishing teaching that the Spirit accomplishes both in him and every believer exactly all that it did in Christ:

> If the Spirit of him who raised Jesus from the dead dwells in you, then he who raised Christ from the dead will bring your mortal bodies to life also, through his Spirit dwelling in you [Rom. 8:11].

Notice in this phrase the triple use of the Spirit: It is the Spirit of the Father, the Spirit in Jesus, and the Spirit in the believing community.

The Spirit Paul experiences is not an impersonal powerful divine force. To the very contrary, it is the love of God himself in action. In the Hebrew Scriptures, *hesed,* or covenant love, is the supreme attribute or quality of God. This love is not merely individual, but a love that goes out to every creature in the universe, especially men and women. It is a love that is not conditioned or qualified by any response that a person might make; it is completely unconditional and unreserved. For this reason, Paul describes the Spirit as the great carrier of God's love to the world and to each person's heart: "The love of God has been poured out in our hearts through the Holy Spirit who has been given to us" (Rom. 5:6).

Paul sees Christ himself as the full embodiment of this outflowing love of God. He sees Christ's love as this great unconditional love of God because it has gone out not just to the good and just but to those who were sinners and had done nothing to deserve it: "It is precisely in this that God proves his love for us: that while we were still sinners, Christ died for us" (Rom. 5:8). For Paul, love and Spirit are interchangeable. They are the driving force of his life. When he writes of his identity with Christ, in the words, "Christ is living in me," he immediately sees this in terms of love, by adding, "It is a life of faith in the Son of God, who loved me and gave himself for me" (Gal. 2:20).

Paul's Lifestyle—The Lifestyle of Jesus

Identity with Christ is not only interior and mystical; it is a new concrete way of living based on the lifestyle of Jesus of Nazareth. Paul could sincerely say, "Imitate me as I imitate Christ" (1 Cor. 11:1). Paul could summarize this lifestyle of Jesus by one word: love. He calls the Christian lifestyle by the name, "the rule of love" (Rom. 14:15). This is brought out in detail when he writes to the Galatians as follows: "The whole law has found its fulfillment in this one saying: 'You shall love your neighbor as yourself' " (Gal. 5:16). He also calls it the "Law of Christ" (Gal. 6:2). He expresses it in a similar form in the letter to the Romans, by writing:

> Owe no debt to anyone except the debt that binds us to love one another. He who loves his neighbor has fulfilled the law. The commandments, "You shall not commit adultery; you shall not murder; you shall not steal; you shall not covet," and any other commandment there may be are all summed up in this, "You shall love your neighbor as yourself." Love never does any wrong to the neighbor, hence love is the fulfillment of the law [Rom. 13:8–10].

Paul can write that love of one's neighbor summarizes everything, because he has deeply experienced that this love is nothing more than a participation in God's own great love for all people, poured into them by the Holy Spirit.

Yet Paul is not content just to use the term "love." He takes pains to spell out that this is an unusual, extraordinary type of love taught by Jesus himself. This is the love even of enemies as taught by Jesus in the Sermon on the

Mount and in his own life. It is a response to injuries, persecution, and even hatred in the form of a beautiful nonviolent love that continually surprises and amazes the world. In his own experience as an apostle, Paul was often insulted, slandered, put in prison, and even tortured. Yet he could say, "When we are insulted, we respond with a blessing" (1 Cor. 4:12). Paul was always struck by Jesus' love, even for those who betrayed him. When writing of the Lord's supper and trying to convey its meaning as a feast of sharing and love, he notes that Jesus' action of love took place "on the night in which he was betrayed" (1 Cor. 11:23).

This love of Jesus, especially shown to Judas and those who betrayed him, must have been especially meaningful to Paul. His deepest sorrow was that many of his own Jewish brothers bitterly opposed him because they could not accept his stand on receiving Gentile converts without the obligation of the biblical laws about circumcision and other traditional observances. It is with sadness that he writes, "Five times at the hands of the Jews I received forty lashes less one" (2 Cor. 11:24). Then there were the "false brothers," the very Christians he had converted who tried to undermine his work (2 Cor. 11:26). These experiences did not make him bitter, but were actually his greatest teachers. They taught him to draw deeply on the Spirit within, the source of loving forgiveness.

So great is Paul's love for his people that he writes to the Romans, "Indeed, I would even wish to be separated from Christ for the sake of my brothers, my kinsmen the Israelites" (Rom. 9:3). On one occasion, when Paul was openly attacked in his absence by a Corinthian leader, it was the cause of great suffering for him. Yet he wrote the Corinthians to take special pains to show their forgiving love for him: "You should now relent and support him so that he may not be crushed by too great a weight of sorrow. I therefore beg you to reaffirm your love for him" (2 Cor. 2:7–8). When Paul wrote to his communities about love, he could speak from personal experience.

"Bless your persecutors; bless and do not curse them" (Rom. 12:14). "Be kind to one another, compassionate, and mutually forgiving, just as God has forgiven you in Christ" (Eph. 4:32).

A great characteristic of Jesus himself was his special love and interest in the poor, the outcasts, the sick, the weak, the lowly. On one occasion, after inviting Levi, a tax-collector, to be an apostle, and after having dinner with other tax-collectors and sinners, Jesus had proclaimed, "People who are healthy do not need a doctor; sick people do. I have come to call sinners, not the self-righteous" (Mark 2:17). Paul was especially moved by this quality of Jesus' love. Wherever possible in his letters, he shows that consideration for the weak is a sure test of the sincerity of love. For example, both in Corinth and in Rome there were some wavering Christians who did not feel they could eat meats that had been previously offered in sacrifice to idols. This was true of practically all meats sold in markets or restaurants. Paul writes, "Extend a kind welcome to those who are weak in faith" (Rom. 14:1). He sees this as a real imitation of Jesus himself, who tried to build up others, especially the weak and sinners.

> We who are strong in faith should be patient with the scruples of those whose faith is weak; we must not be selfish. Each should please his neighbor so as to do him good by building up his spirit. Thus in accord with Scripture, Christ did not please himself [Rom. 15:1–3].

Paul has a real sympathy and understanding for the weak. He could truthfully say, "To the weak I became a weak person with a view of winning the weak" (1 Cor. 9:22).

There are some other indications that Paul knew and practiced Jesus' teachings on love as found in the Sermon on the Mount. Jesus emphasized the nonjudgmental nature of love when he declared, "If you want to avoid judgment, stop passing judgment" (Matt. 7:1). Paul gives special attention to this quality of love. In writing to the Galatians, he emphasizes that they should try to help sinners by gentle and helpful advice, carefully avoiding comparisons or judgment.

> My brothers, if someone is detected in sin, you who live by the spirit should gently set him right, each of you trying to avoid falling into temptation himself. Help carry one another's burdens; in that way you will fulfill the law of Christ. If anyone thinks he amounts to something, when in fact he is nothing, he is only deceiving himself [Gal. 6:1–3].

In reference to the Christians who were divided as to the matter of eating foods sacrificed to others, Paul confronts both groups by writing, "Every one of us will have to give an account of himself before God. Therefore we must no longer pass judgment on one another" (Rom. 14:12–13).

Jesus had taught that the ordinary laws of justice and retribution were not sufficient. A new law of love was necessary, a love that was nonresistant and won others by replying to injuries and even lawsuits by generosity and surprising favors even to oppressors. "What I say to you is: offer no resistance to injury. When a person strikes you on the right cheek, turn and offer him the other. If anyone wants to go to law over your shirt, hand him your coat as well" (Matt. 5:39–40).

Paul does not regard this attitude as merely an idea, but as something that is to be seen in daily life. He was quite shocked to learn that Corinthians were going to ordinary civil courts to settle their disputes. In the first place, he asks why they cannot come to agreement and reconciliation by discussing the matter within the community. "Must brother drag brother into court, and before unbelievers at that?'' (1 Cor. 6:6). Then he asks why they do not willingly accept injury and win over others through love, rather than through retribution: ''Why, the very fact that you have lawsuits against one another is disastrous for you. Why not put up with injustice, and let yourselves be cheated?'' (1 Cor. 6:7)

Jesus—God's Humble Servant in Paul

Paul's image of Jesus was that of a man so transfixed and permeated by the Spirit of God that his entire life was dedicated to letting God's light and love shine through him to others in loving service. Since Paul felt he was intimately identified with Jesus, this image became deeply imbedded in him. Paul likes to describe himself simply as a servant of God or as a servant of others. ''It is not ourselves that we preach but Christ Jesus as Lord, and ourselves as your servants for Jesus' sake'' (2 Cor. 4:5). Also, ''men should regard us as servants of Christ and administrators of the mysteries of God'' (1 Cor. 4:1).

Paul's favorite and most moving picture of Jesus as the humble servant of God is found in an ancient Christian hymn which he must have sung and repeated to himself again and again. When Paul learned that there was division and squabbling within the Philippians' community, he wrote to remind them to adopt the attitude of Christ and serve one another, looking to each other's interests rather than their own. He did this in the form of a song which he presumes they were familiar with. The first part is as follows:

> Though he was in the form of God
> he did not deem equality with God
> something to be grasped at.
> Rather he emptied himself
> and took the form of a slave,
> being born in the likeness of men.
> He was known to be of human estate

and it was thus that he humbled himself,
obediently accepting even death,
death on a cross!
Because of this,
God highly exalted him
and bestowed on him the name
above every other name [Phil. 2:6–9].

In view of this striking image, Paul saw the human body as an instrument of loving service which could be united to the body of Christ as a devoted sacrifice to God: "Brothers, I beg you through the mercy of God to offer your bodies as a living sacrifice holy and acceptable to God, your spiritual worship" (Rom. 12:1).

I noted that Paul must have sung the hymn of the humble servant many times because of the importance of song in the early Christian community as a means of expressing oneness and identity with Christ. The letter to the Colossians has this advice: "Sing gratefully to God from your heart in psalms, hymns, and inspired songs" (Col. 3:16). The letter to the Ephesians states, "Be filled with the Spirit, addressing one another in psalms and hymns and inspired songs" (Eph. 5:19). Writing to the Corinthians, Paul notes that the members might have a song to share with the community: "When you assemble, one has a psalm, another some instruction to give, still another a revelation to share" (1 Cor. 14:26). In his Acts of the Apostles, Luke notes that the singing of Paul and his companions made such an impression on their fellow prisoners that all were listening intently to them until midnight (Acts 16:25).

For Paul, the image of the humble servant was summed up by the words, "for you," or "for your sakes." It was an expression that summarized Jesus' own ideal of complete dedication to the service of the world. This came to a climax and had its most visible expression in the eucharistic offering: "This is my body, which is for you" (1 Cor. 11:24; cf. Luke 22:19). Paul felt that these words should be his motto also as he wrote to the Corinthians:

> While we live we are constantly being delivered
> to death for Jesus' sake, so that the life of Jesus
> may be revealed in our mortal flesh. Death is at
> work in us, but life in you [2 Cor. 4:11–12].
> . . . Indeed, everything is ordered to your benefit [literally, ''Everything is for your sakes''; 2
> Cor. 4:15].

To sum up: Identity with Christ was Paul's great secret. The Spirit of Christ was his own Spirit and gave him a new principle of activity, life, and energy, in place of his previous trust in his own achievements and will power. This Spirit was essentially a Spirit of love that prompted Paul to imitate closely the lifestyle of Jesus himself as exemplified in the Sermon on the Mount and in his ministry to the weak, the suffering, and sinners. It was summed up in the ideal and image of the humble servant of God as found in an ancient Christian song.

Reflections for Modern Christians

Paul could well understand our modern world with its tremendous emphasis on advancement, achievement, and progress. He had gone through it all in his life as a Pharisee, even though he was well-motivated. It was a shock and change to him, as it will be to you, when he found that the important matter is not achievement, but surrender to a new principle of energy, power, and love: the Spirit of God as found in union and identity with Jesus. This Spirit is a Spirit of love; it is God's own love in action as manifested through you. It is no longer a question so much of *what you do but what you are within. What you do* will be this inner principle of life and love in action: It will be the lifestyle of Jesus duplicated again in your daily life. As such, it will provide continual surprises to people in the world around you, for it will be a nonviolent love that wins over others through peace, reconciliation, and forgiveness.

A love that is from God the Holy Spirit is a love that accepts and loves the people and world around you *as they are,* not as you might want them to be. A deep, true love for the world is essential to any apostle who hopes to transform it. This is the continuation of the love of Jesus for the poor, the needy, the sick, the outcasts, and the sinners. It cannot be a love for the world in the abstract, but a love for the world in its concrete reality; a love for it in all its strength and all its weakness. God himself proved his love for the world by sending his Son to help people in their actual condition: "God proves his love for us: that while we were still sinners, Christ died for us" (Rom. 5:8).

This love for the world must be experienced in view of all its practical consequences. It means being open to all its values and goodness. And this means listening to the world as it is today with all its needs and problems. It means being alert to the particular contribution of each culture; it means a real appreciation of what people have done in science, education, government, industry, and art. When I say "world," I do not mean a lifeless globe but the teeming masses of humanity that make up the world. The world needs to be loved as it is. Those joined to Christ, and identified with him, are joined to the great love of God for the world that was and is in Jesus.

All of this will result in accepting joyfully the humble role of servant, a role that was Christ's and Paul's. It will establish a new direction, an outflow movement in life that will continually touch the center of love in other people. This will result in frequent surprises as this bounces back to you unexpectedly from so many sides each day. It will be contagious by its very nature. It is really not anything you do or say. Somehow, *who you are* and the meaning of your life will come across to others in countless ways no matter what your occupation, profession, or work may be. This outflow movement will continually give you more energy. Most of your energy is lost through a protective, defensive movement that is looking to your own interests. Once this is surrendered and given up then all that energy will be released and vitality will be increased. Once you "give it all up," surprisingly, you "get it all back."

A striking living example of the identity with Christ that Paul spoke about and lived had its beginning in August 1948 in Calcutta, India. A young woman from Yugoslavia had just finished teaching twenty years at a private high school. Although the convent and school were in the midst of hopeless destitution and poverty, it was an oasis of beauty, cleanliness, and reasonable comfort. One day, while riding on a train, she felt the urgent call to take seriously Christ's own love for the poor and abandoned. She left her teaching order and began to minister to men and women sick and dying on the streets of Calcutta. Her name is now known throughout the world as Mother Teresa of Calcutta. She was able to acquire a building that could house the hopeless cases that hospitals were not able to accommodate. Soon other men and women began to join her in her selfless imitation of Christ. It did not matter what religion they professed; she required only love for the poor and dying. This, she felt, was needed more than physical attention. Since then the work of her new community of men and women has spread to new centers among the poor all over the world. Her motto, which she keeps repeating, is the words of Paul in Galatians 2:20, "The life I live now is not my own; Christ is living in me." Mother Teresa does not take any credit for what she does. She only feels that it is Christ's own love for the poor that works through her and others.

3

Identification with Others: Worker for One World

In Christ: The Model for One World

For Paul, identity with Christ was not only, or even primarily an individual matter. To be "in Christ" meant to be part of a community that shared his Spirit. It also meant to be a part of a whole inner movement in the world that was directed to creating a new oneness in humanity. This was a direction in God's plan ever since creation when he had formed man and woman to his own image and likeness as his own family on earth. To believe in one God was to believe in one family of humankind—a family that could overcome the many barriers of separation that had grown up over the countless centuries during which people became scattered over all the earth and divided from one another.

The expression "in Christ" or its equivalent is found some 164 times in Paul's letters. It is his favorite expression to express a new union and solidarity of people under the leadership of Jesus. This union is made possible by a sharing of the one Spirit of God in Christ. This sharing took place through an opening or surrender in faith that was represented and symbolized by baptism. Paul was convinced that God's great secret and long hidden plan to bring the world together again was revealed through Christ. The Apostle felt that it was his great privilege to make this secret known and become a dedicated worker for oneness in the world.

In his letter to the Romans, Paul sees an inner divine movement in all of creation that is moving men and women to a final unity where they will all be part of God's family, children of God in the fullest possible manner.

> Indeed, the whole created world eagerly awaits the revelation of the sons of God. . . . The world itself will be freed from its slavery to corruption and share in the glorious freedom of the children of God. Yes, we know that all creation groans and is in agony even until now [Rom. 8:20–22].

These groans are the groans of the earth-mother waiting to give birth to the new age when all humankind and all creation will be once more one. The powerful agent of oneness is the one Spirit of God: "All who are led by the Spirit of God are sons of God" (Rom. 8:14). The inner movement of the Spirit is so powerful that there is a coordinating and directive movement within human history to make this possible: "We know that God makes all things work together for the good of those who have been called according to his decree" (Rom. 8:26).

In Paul's letter to the Colossians, we find a beautiful development of his thought on the whole matter of world unity. He describes a great cosmic plan of God to bring the world together through Christ. Paul sees Christ as already existing in God from the beginning of creation as a center of power and energy to unify and bring together the entire universe:

> He is the image of the Invisible God, the first-born of all creatures. In him everything in heaven and on earth was created, things visible and invisible, whether thrones or domina-

tions, principalities or powers; all were created
through him, and for him. He is before all else
that is. In him everything continues in being
[Col. 1:15–17].

This, however, is a hidden mystery. The actual condition
of most people is that they have become alienated from
God and from one another. They have lost knowledge of
this inner principle of oneness and unity: "You yourselves were once alienated from him; you nourished
hostility in your hearts because of your evil deeds"
(Col. 1:21).

This alienation has affected the universe in which we
live. It has also created disunity within the various powers of the universe that Paul calls the "principalities and
powers." God's great plan is to reconcile the world and
bring it together once more. "But now Christ has
achieved reconciliation for you in his mortal body by
dying, so as to present you to God, holy, free of reproach
and blame" (Col. 1:22). The dying of Christ was a voluntary severing from all the hostile, separating powers of
sin in the world in order to make possible a new beginning. This new beginning took place as all the fullness of
God's power present in Christ was transferred to a
church, a community of believers who shared Christ's
power and Spirit.

It is he who is head of the body, the church; he
who is the beginning, the first born of the dead,
so that primacy may be his in everything. It
pleased God to make absolute fullness reside in
him and, by means of him, to reconcile everything in his person, both on earth and in the
heavens, making peace through the blood of the
cross [Col. 1:18–20].

Paul feels that he has been given an unusual and precious privilege in being chosen to be a minister and agent to the world of this great mystery of unity:

> I became a minister of this church through the commission God gave me to preach among you his word in its fullness, that mystery hidden from ages and generations past but now revealed to his holy ones. God has willed to make known to them the glory beyond price which this mystery brings to the Gentiles—the mystery of Christ in you, your hope of glory [Col. 1:25–26].

The Removal of the Social Roots of Disunity in Humankind

The unity that Paul writes about is not merely idealistic or internal. It began immediately to break down the very evident social and cultural barriers that separated people in the ancient world. This is implied in the above verses where Paul especially emphasizes that the Gentiles, the non-Jewish world, have the mystery of Christ working within them. This would appear strange to them because the hope of a Christ, or Messiah, was essentially a Jewish one, yet now both Jews and Gentiles could be united under the same appointed leaders from God.

This social implication is more carefully spelled out in the letter to the Ephesians. The Gentiles in the course of history had become estranged and separated from the Jews, originally members of the same human family:

> In former times, you had no part in Christ and were excluded from the community of Israel. You were strangers to the covenant and its promise: You were without hope and without God in the world [Eph. 2:12].

The great barrier of separation was the Law with all its

observances, especially circumcision and regulations
that made any real fellowship between Jew and Gentile
virtually impossible. A visible symbol of this separation
was the Berlin Wall of the day, which was a wall in the
Temple area that forbade any Gentiles from going further
under penalty of death. Paul sees the great work of Christ
as the breaking down of the great wall of separation that
divided the ancient world into two parts, Gentile and
Jew.

> But now in Christ Jesus you who once were far
> off have been brought near through the blood of
> Christ. It is he who is our peace, and who made
> the two of us one by breaking down the barrier of
> hostility that kept us apart [Eph. 2:14].

The ultimate goal was to create a new oneness in humanity, a "new person" who could be joined together by the
same Holy Spirit and thus together approach the one
God:

> . . . to create in himself one new man from us
> who had been two and to make peace, reconcil-
> ing both of us to God in one body through his
> cross. . . . Through him we both have access in
> one Spirit to the Father. This means that you are
> strangers and aliens no longer. No, you are fel-
> low citizens of the saints and members of the
> household of God [Eph. 2:15–18].

Paul ends with the startling statement that all humanity
can thus become one great new Temple of God. No other
structures are needed:

> You form a building which rises on the founda-
> tion of the apostles and prophets, with Christ
> Jesus himself as the capstone. Through him the
> whole structure is fitted together and takes

shape as a holy temple in the Lord; in him
you are being built into this temple, to become
a dwelling place for God in the Spirit [Eph.
2:20–22].

The author is so enthusiastic about the beautiful Spirit of
oneness he has experienced that he composes a poem
with a sevenfold theme of oneness—seven being a
number of fullness that represents the universality of
God's Spirit.

There is but one body and one Spirit, just as
there is but one hope given all of you by your call.
There is one Lord, one faith, one baptism; one
God and Father of all, who is over all and works
through all, and is in all [Eph. 4:4–6].

The Local Church as Model for Oneness in the World

In this vision, what is the place of the local church, or
community of believers? For Paul, it is the visible image
and model of what the Spirit of oneness wants to accomplish in the whole world. The church is meant to be a little
world that tells the larger world what is going on within
it, and what is to be its goal. For this reason, Paul understands baptism as the clothing over with Christ of the
new person who breaks down the social barriers between
Jew and Greek, slave and freeman, male and female.
These were the three great "class" barriers in the ancient
world.

All of you who have been baptized into Christ
have clothed yourselves with him. There does
not exist among you Jew or Greek, slave or
freeman, male or female. All are one in Christ
Jesus [Gal. 3:27–28].

More will be said about this social aspect in Chapter 7, on the gospel of freedom. Paul saw the local church as the model for the elimination of segregation and inequality that should take place in the whole world.

In the letter to the Colossians, this social aspect is emphasized even more strongly. Baptism is a separation from the old self, the old humanity where selfishness, separation, and segregation were so evident. Instead, a new person is put on, a new person according to the image of God that was destined for humanity in creation (Gen. 1:27). This new person is a new united humanity. It is now like God our Father who is supreme oneness:

> What you have done is put aside your old self with its past deeds and put on a new man, one who grows in knowledge as he is formed anew in the image of his Creator. There is no Greek or Jew here, circumcised or uncircumcised, foreigner, Scythian, slave or freeman. Rather, Christ is everything in all of you [Col. 3:9–11].

The theme of oneness and identification with others reaches its best expression in the description of the church as the one body of Christ. Whether a person was of a different race or social class made no difference at all. The same basic life-giving principle, the Spirit of God, was in all of them to such an extent that their oneness is like that existing in a human body.

> The body is one and has many members, but all the members, many though they are, are one body; and so it is with Christ. It was in one Spirit that all of us, whether Jew or Greek, slave or free, were baptized into one body. All of us have been given to drink of the one Spirit [1 Cor. 12:12–13].

Likewise it makes no difference what talent or gift a person has. The source of all gifts, the Holy Spirit, is the same. And since it is the same, whatever is given is given not as a private benefit but for the good of all, who are one body because of the Spirit. To express this unity as strongly as possible, Paul uses a trinitarian ladder, the Spirit, the Lord (Christ, son and source of the Spirit), and God (the Father):

> There are different gifts but the same Spirit; there are different ministries but the same Lord; there are different works but the same God who accomplishes all of them in everyone. To each person the manifestation of the Spirit is given for the common good [1 Cor. 12:4–7].

Because of this basic oneness, the principal community gathering, the celebration of the Lord's Supper or Eucharist, centered about eating and drinking bread and wine as signifying their oneness in the body of the Risen Christ:

> Is not the cup of blessing we bless a sharing in the blood of Christ? And is not the bread we break a sharing in the body of Christ? Because the loaf of bread is one, we, many though we are, are one body, for we all partake of the one loaf [1 Cor. 10:16–17].

Every celebration of the Lord's Supper was meant to deepen and express this basic unity in Christ by the closest possible unity with him and one another. The "breaking of bread" was an ancient symbol of covenant and unity. The sharing of one cup was called the cup of covenant, so much so that marriage vows were sealed by bride and groom sharing the same cup of wine. As the community ate the bread, their thoughts turned to God the source of all bread and nourishment, now shown especially through Jesus his son. As they drank the wine, they thought of the many grapes who had given their lifeblood to make the new sparkling wine possible. They thought of the death of Christ who had given his life in order to share his Spirit with them, so that all might be united together in the new wine of the Spirit like so many grapes.

Paul's one great goal in life was to create permanent community among men and women. According to the custom of his time, whenever he taught, his disciples sat around him in the form of a semi-circle or crown. For this reason, Jewish teachers spoke of their disciples as being their crown. Paul sees the community he has formed as a permanent crown filled with God's glory and Spirit that will last forever and be rejoined with him at the end of history:

> Who, after all, if not you, will be our hope or joy, or the crown we exult in, before our Lord Jesus Christ at his coming? You are our boast and our delight [1 Thess. 2:19–20].

Oneness and the Sharing of Food ' and Material Goods

Besides its spiritual and social aspects the theme of oneness had an important economic dimension also. If they were really one in the Spirit, one in the Lord, they were a family of brothers and sisters. It was unthinkable that some might have a superabundance of material goods and others have little or be destitute. That is why Paul was greatly alarmed when he heard news about the way that some Christians were celebrating the Last Supper of Jesus.

> What I now have to say is not said in praise, because your meetings are not profitable but harmful. First of all, I hear that when you gather for a meeting there are divisions among you, and I am inclined to believe it [1 Cor. 11:17–18].

Paul was so disturbed that he could even tell the Christians that their holiest gatherings were harmful! The divisions he speaks about can be understood in the light of Christian customs of the time. Before celebrating their Eucharist, or Supper of the Lord, the community had a common meal together. It resembled a picnic where each family or household brought along the food they needed. Some of the richer households prepared sumptuous and expensive banquets and had liquor and wine in plentiful supply. Other poor families had bread and scanty provisions.

Paul is so surprised by this practice that he tells them, "When you assemble it is not to eat the Lord's Supper, for everyone is in haste to eat his own supper. One person goes hungry while another gets drunk" (1 Cor. 11:20). Paul sees this abuse as directly opposed to what it means to be a true community or church. In addition it is a direct insult and embarrassment to the poor: "Would you show contempt for the church of God, and embarrass those who have nothing?" (1 Cor. 11:22). Most important of all, the Corinthian practice was in direct contrast to the inner nature of the Last Supper of Jesus. This was in essence a celebration of the self-giving of Jesus even as far as death. Consequently, Paul draws special attention to Jesus' death as he recalls the tradition of Jesus' last supper.

> I received from the Lord what I handed on to you, namely, that the Lord Jesus on the night on which he was betrayed took bread, and after he had given thanks, broke it and said, "This is my body, which is for you. Do this in remembrance of me" [1 Cor. 11:25].

Paul takes special note of the night of betrayal, because what Jesus did was pure unconditional love even in the face of betrayal by his best friends. The words "my body which is for you" especially emphasize the essential element of self-giving love. The eating of bread, the body of Christ, is a pledge of imitation of Jesus and communion with him in this action of self-giving love. The words "do this in remembrance of me" show that Jesus himself wanted to be remembered in this way so Christians might experience his presence in the deepest possible manner as they unite their lives to his in an expression of love for others even unto death.

"In the same way, after the supper, he took the cup, saying 'This cup is the new covenant in my blood.' " The common sharing of the cup strengthens and intensifies the meaning of the shared bread. The blood of Jesus once again emphasizes the essential place of his death as the supreme act of love toward which his life moved. "Every time, then, you eat this bread and drink this cup, you proclaim the death of the Lord until he comes" (1 Cor. 11:26). Paul sees the whole action as a public proclamation to the world of their desire to take upon themselves the meaning of the death of Jesus in their lives in the world. Thus it was extremely important that this ritual action have full meaning in the lives of the participators. "This means that whoever eats the bread or drinks the cup of the Lord unworthily sins against the body and blood of the Lord" (1 Cor. 11:27). Because of this responsibility, Paul asks that all seriously examine their lives or judge themselves before taking part in the Last Supper celebration: "A man should examine himself first; only then should he eat of the bread and drink of the cup" (1 Cor. 11:28).

Paul is convinced that there can be no meaningful ritual celebration if there is no real sharing between rich and poor in the common meals of Christians. That is why he can write, "He who eats and drinks without recognizing the body eats and drinks a judgment on himself!" (1 Cor. 11:29). Our author was deeply convinced that lack of honesty and commitment in relationships with others had psychosomatic effects also. The separation from brothers and sisters in need produced anxiety, worry, and physical effects as well. So he can state, "That is why many among you are sick and infirm and why so many are dying" (1 Cor. 11:30). When this happens, Paul does not see it as a disaster, but as an opportunity to learn a lesson that comes from God himself. Those who learn and reorient their lives will receive a blessing that comes as a result of this suffering and anxiety.

> If we were to examine ourselves we would not be falling under judgment in this way; but since it is the Lord who judges us, he chastens us to keep us from being condemned with the rest of the world [1 Cor. 11:31–32].

Paul then makes a final practical application to correct the abuses in the eucharistic celebrations: "Therefore, my brothers, when you assemble for the meal, wait for one another. If anyone is hungry, let him eat at home, so that your assembly may not deserve condemnation" (1 Cor. 11:34). The celebration of the Eucharist and the spiritual sharing of the bread and wine cannot be divorced from a practical sharing of material goods and a real concern for the poor, needy, and hungry.

The Ecumenical Collection Among the Gentile Churches for the Jewish Poor

During his entire apostolate, the project closest to Paul's heart was that of a weekly collection among all the churches he had established in Asia Minor and Europe. The immediate purpose was to send material assistance to both Jews and Jewish Christians in Israel. However, beyond this, it was meant to be an extraordinary sign of the new oneness in the world that was made possible by the gospel. What he was doing was simply unbelievable and unheard of in the ancient world with its long history of separation and animosity between Gentile and Jew. This sharing would show the world, and the church in

Jerusalem, that the Gentiles were truly their spiritual brothers and sisters despite all the impossible barriers of race, religion, and culture that had been built up over the centuries. It was truly an ecumenical collection.

This great collection for the poor is mentioned in all the major letters of Paul. The idea seems to have first started when Paul made an agreement with Peter that the latter was to be an apostle to the Jewish world, while Paul was to concentrate on the Gentiles. The great concern of the early church was that unity and oneness be preserved despite this separate approach to Jews and Gentiles. It was suggested that a collection among the richer Gentile churches would be a concrete sign of the brotherhood and oneness made possible by the gospel.

> Those who were the acknowledged pillars, James, Cephas, and John, gave Barnabas and me the handclasp of fellowship, signifying that we should go to the Gentiles as they to the Jews. The only stipulation was that we should be mindful of the poor—the one thing that I was making every effort to do [Gal. 2:9–10].

In reference to the collection, Paul gave the following instructions to the Corinthians:

> About the collection for the saints, follow the instructions I gave the churches of Galatia. On the first day of each week everyone should put aside whatever he has been able to save, so that the collection will not have to be taken up after I arrive [1 Cor. 16:1–2].

Paul asked that delegates from each of the churches accompany the money to Jerusalem so that it would be a real personal offering of love from the Gentile churches: "When I come I shall give letters of introduction to those whom you have chosen to take your gift to Jerusalem. If it seems fitting that I should go myself, they will accompany me" (1 Cor. 16:3–4).

Paul devotes two chapters of Second Corinthians to the subject of this important collection. Of special interest is his emphasis on equality and sharing as central to the gospel.

> The relief of others ought not to impoverish you; there should be a certain equality. Your plenty at the present time should supply their need so that their surplus may one day supply your need, with equality as the result [2 Cor. 8:14].

Paul feels that God's gifts are meant for everyone, especially food. Consequently, it should be equally shared. As an example of this equal distribution of God's gifts, Paul recalls the story of God's provision of manna, or miraculous bread, to the Israelites in the desert (Exod. 16). When this manna fell to the ground, all went out and gathered it, young and old, strong and weak. But despite the fact that some gathered more than others, it was equally divided among all at the end of the day. In reference to this story Paul writes, "It is written, 'He who gathered much had no excess and he who gathered little had no lack' " (2 Cor. 8:15).

Paul was convinced that the sharing of spiritual blessings and faith must be accompanied by the sharing of material blessings as well. He brings this out in Romans 15:25–27:

> Just now I am leaving for Jerusalem to bring assistance to the saints. Macedonia and Achaia have kindly decided to make a contribution for those in need among the saints in Jerusalem. They did so of their own accord, yet they are also under obligation. For if the Gentiles have shared in the spiritual blessings of the Jews, they ought to contribute to their temporal needs in return.

Identification with Others: The Feeling Level

Paul's experience of Christ was not only spiritual but reached the deepest level of his feelings as well. His strong heartfelt love of Christ made him ready to risk every kind of danger, even death itself: "Who will separate us from the love of Christ? Trial, distress, or persecution, or hunger, or nakedness, or danger, or the sword?" (Rom. 8:35). The love of Christ was so great and all-embracing that no power in the universe could tear Paul away from the love of God that he experienced in Jesus.

> For I am certain that neither death nor life, neither angels nor principalities, neither the present nor the future, nor powers, neither height nor depth nor any other creature, will be able to separate us from the love of God that comes to us in Christ Jesus, our Lord [Rom. 8:38–39].

What was true of Paul's identity with Christ was true of his relationship with others: It reached the deep feeling level also. His letters are filled with expressions of love and affection for his Christians. Paul himself had taught them that in every Christian meeting there should be an affectionate embrace, a "kiss of peace": "Greet one another with a holy kiss" (1 Cor. 16:20; 2 Cor. 13:12; Rom. 16:16).

In his teachings, some of this deep level of sensitivity and identification with others comes out strongly. Paul was especially concerned about the "weak" Christians at Rome and Corinth who were still afraid to eat meats that had been associated with idol offerings. He writes to the "strong" that they should have a deep sensitivity for the "weak":

> Because of your "knowledge" the weak one perishes, that brother for whom Christ died.

When you sin thus against your brothers and wound their weak consciences, you are sinning against Christ [1 Cor. 8:11–12].

In describing the relationship between Christians in the "body of Christ," he is careful to describe how they deeply affect one another and need one another: "If one member suffers, all the members suffer with it; if one member is honored, all the members share its joy" (1 Cor. 12:26). In fact it is God's special plan and desire that each person have a unique gift that is needed by others so there can be a beautiful interdependence and concern for one another: ". . . that all the members may be concerned for one another" (1 Cor. 12:25). Paul sees this spirit of close identification with others on the feeling level as an essential part of Christian life. In his brief summary of Christian living in Romans 12, he writes, "Rejoice with those who rejoice, weep with those who weep. Have the same attitude toward all. Put away ambitious thoughts and associate with the lowly" (Rom. 12:15–16).

To sum up: "In Christ," for Paul, had a special community meaning. He understood it as a powerful inner movement in himself and in all human history directing the world to unity and oneness. Paul saw this as pulling down the great social, racial, and cultural barriers that divided humanity. The role of the local church was to be a visible model and image of what the Spirit of God wanted in the whole world. The spirit of Christ was the source of a deep spiritual and emotional oneness that meant equality and sharing between rich and poor, slave and freeman, male and female, Jew and foreigner.

Application for Modern Christians

It is easy to notice that many people lack a sense of real meaning, purpose, and direction in life. This results in a sense of boredom and heaviness. It also entails much unnecessary suffering, as people strive so hard to fill up that emptiness with satisfactions and pleasures that offer only a brief respite from an enduring sense of futility. Others try to escape through alcohol, drugs, and other "cop-outs" only to return to face reality with diminished and weakened resources.

There can be no substitute for going deep within life itself as you search for meaning. Nothing "outside" can satisfy your quest. Deep within you will find the Spirit, the mystery of Christ. It is a Spirit of oneness that gives a new sense of direction and purpose to your life and that of the world. As you surrender in faith to this inner core of your being and that of others you will find a surprising source of energy, strength, and power for your life. You will find a "sacrament of each moment," because you will find in each happening, each encounter, all you need to be really happy. You will not be distracted by memories of the past, or dreams about the future. This is because you will have found within you and within life itself all you really need.

Like Paul, you will discover that the Spirit is love itself. Since this Spirit is shared by others, your life will become more and more person-centered. This will take place as you reverence the mystery within each person instead of regarding others as objects or means for some end. This mystery will draw you to form with others a real community where sharing is not only spiritual but emotional, social, and economic. You will find yourself working more and more for all that promotes true equality and fellowship with others, despite differences of race, color, creed, or culture. In all this you will be gently moved by the great Spirit of oneness that is working within the human family wherever you go.

Openness to the Spirit will make you want to duplicate, like Paul, the lifestyle of Jesus himself. In doing so, you will embrace the role of a humble servant, who sees himself as a part of one great divine plan. Thus you will find happiness in loving and serving others in any way you can. You will regard yourself as a holy vessel of the Spirit, which will want to radiate God's love in and through you. The special quality of this love will be that of Jesus, a nonviolent, selfless, unconditional love that breaks down the barriers of separation between people by disarming their defensiveness.

As you find yourself more and more "in Christ," you will treasure the mutual support of a smaller community that will be an image and model of what the Spirit wants to do in the whole world. It will not be a community of "elite" or perfect, but one that welcomes and accepts people as they are, just as Jesus did. It will be a community that is Spirit-centered, supporting one another through prayer and encouragement. In their gatherings you will experience a certain fullness of the Spirit as each one's gift, love, and concern becomes yours as well, since the Spirit is one.

Those recognizing like Paul the Spirit of God in every movement toward oneness, whether social, economic, or religious, will try to be ever alert to seek out and cooperate with those persons or groups who are actively working toward that end. With this in mind, a careful reading even of the newspapers can lead to quite surprising and unexpected results. It would not be the function of this book to provide a list of names and addresses. However, some examples can be given. Those interested in imitating Paul's deep concern for oneness in sharing food and material resources can contact *Bread for the World* (207 East 16th Street, New York, NY 10003). Those who wish to collaborate with small communities or groups of persons combatting social injustice in various parts of the world can find considerable information in *The National Catholic Reporter* (Box 281, Kansas City, MO 64141). There is a veritable mine of information on resources and people working effectively to break the social, religious, economic, and racial barriers that separate people in *The Patriot's Bible* (Orbis Books, Maryknoll, NY 10545). The *Christophers* (12 East 48th St., New York, NY

10017) send a monthly news note free of charge to those interested in being effective agents of change and responsibility in today's world.

4

Teamworker for Christ

In our last chapter, we have just seen how Paul was most anxious that the local community itself be a model, beginning, and example of what the Spirit wanted to do in the world. As a preparation for this, Paul was not a lone apostle. He and his companions already were a miniature church that people could join and stay with until they were able to form their own independent community. Then Paul would feel free to move on.

Paul's Teamworkers: A Traveling Church

The apostle Paul was a teamworker. He saw the special meaning and the great advantages of working with a group of apostles like himself. He took as a guide the example and advice of the Master himself, who sent them out two by two (Mark 6:7). Jesus himself had set the precedent. The community of the twelve was in reality a traveling commune. They lived together, ate together, and shared a common purse. What they did not need for themselves they shared with the poor (John 12:6; 13:29).

A few examples will indicate that Paul was usually accompanied by two or three fellow workers in his journeys and evangelization. On the first missionary journey he was accompanied by Barnabas and Mark (Acts 13–14). Luke describes their work as a group effort; e.g., "they proclaimed the word of God" (14:6). In the letters to the

Thessalonians, it is "Paul and Silvanus and Timothy" who address the church (1 Thess. 1:1; 2 Thess. 2:1). The preaching of the gospel was a joint effort; it is "our preaching of the gospel" (1 Thess. 1:5); "we drew courage from our God to preach his good tidings to you" (1 Thess. 2:2). "We could have insisted on our importance as apostles of Christ" (1 Thess. 2:6). The same was true of the evangelization of Corinth. Paul writes, "Jesus Christ, whom Silvanus, Timothy, and I preached to you as Son of God, was not alternately 'yes' and 'no' " (2 Cor. 1:19). In Ephesus, Titus is a "companion and fellow worker" of Paul (2 Cor. 8:23). Among other coworkers and fellow apostles are Luke (Philemon 24; Col. 4:14; Rom. 16:2), Erastus (Acts 19:22), Aristarchus (Col. 4:10), and Tychicus (Col. 4:7).

Why did Paul consider this teamwork so important? The answer cannot be found in so many words in either the Acts of the Apostles or the Epistles. But reading between the lines, we can note the following points:

1. Since Paul was going to places where the gospel had not yet been preached, he felt it necessary to present a visible picture of the church in action. The group of apostles formed a church in miniature that they could thus invite others to join and thus share the spirit of the risen Jesus. To believe was to join one's self to Christ in union with the inspired group of people who had come among them. When Paul and Silas preached at Thessalonica, Luke writes, "Some of the Jews were convinced and threw in their lot with Paul and Silas" (Acts 17:4). The team was also a visible example of how the gospel was destined to break down the great social and racial barriers that separated humankind. Paul made it a special point usually to have a Jerusalem Jew with him, such as Silas or Barnabas, along with a Gentile, such as Titus, or a half-Gentile such as Timothy. It was enough for people to see Paul and other Jews eating, living, and traveling with Gentiles. It was a visible and striking sign

to the world of the oneness that the power of the Spirit could accomplish.

2. The apostolic team responded to a real need of Paul as a member of the new family which was the church. He never tired of telling his converts to encourage and exhort one another as brothers and sisters so they could remain steadfast in their faith. He repeated this because he felt that need so strongly himself. He found it a real hardship to remain alone. In fact, his greatest failure was at Athens where very few entered the church. Here circumstances forced Paul to preach by himself. He hints as how difficult this was for him in his words to the Thessalonians, "That is why, when we could endure it no longer, we decided to remain alone at Athens, and send Timothy. He is our brother and fellow worker . . . " (1 Thess. 3:1).

The expressions Paul used to describe his companions indicate how much the members of his "apostolic family" meant to him. There was real heartfelt love between them. Of Timothy he wrote to the Philippians,

> I have no one quite like him for genuine interest
> in whatever concerns you. . . . He was like a son
> at his father's side serving the gospel along with
> me   [Phil. 2:20–22].

The Philippians had sent a certain Epaphroditus to assist him. Paul describes him as, "my brother, co-worker, and comrade in arms" (Phil. 2:25). Paul refers to Luke, another companion, as "our dear physician" (Col. 4:14). He describes Tychicus as "our dear brother, our faithful minister, and fellow slave in the Lord" (Col. 4:7). Onesimus had been a slave before becoming Paul's helper. The apostle refers to him as "our dear and faithful brother" (Col. 4:9).

For Paul, the atmosphere of his traveling commune was an important one for his own personal growth.

There were many differences and sources of conflict in this small group. It was a good occasion for them to see one another realistically and to learn to be accepting as well as forgiving. On one occasion there was a serious conflict between Paul and Barnabas when Paul began his second missionary journey (Acts 15:38–39). This was because Paul did not wish to take along Barnabas's cousin Mark, who had deserted them during the first journey. However, we see later that both Paul and Mark had grown through this conflict. In the letter to the Colossians Paul extends a special greeting to Mark. The church there is instructed to receive Mark if he visits (Col. 4:10).

3. The whole group of apostles was able to present a more balanced picture of the church than Paul himself; indeed, at times they were able to save his work when it was endangered as a result of his particular way of presenting the good news. Paul had the gift of assurance and boldness in his preaching. This was a quality that won many converts, but at the same time there were some drawbacks. Perhaps Paul overdid it at times. At Lystra, the crowds stoned Paul, but did not harm Barnabas (Acts 14). At Beroea, the Jews from Thessalonica stirred up the people against Paul, who was forced to make a hasty departure. However, Silas and Timothy stayed on and were able to consolidate work that might have otherwise been lost (Acts 17:10–15). So we see that other members of the apostolic team provided a helpful balance for the somewhat impetuous Paul. The variety of their talents and gifts was a better mirror of the Spirit of God.

4. Paul's traveling school provided a very valuable training opportunity for others who would carry on the same type of work. He himself had served an apprenticeship under Barnabas and knew how much it meant to have a patient guide. It was Barnabas who had first introduced Paul to the Jerusalem community when everyone was afraid to accept him:

> Now when he arrived back in Jerusalem he tried
> to join the disciples there, but it turned out that

they were all afraid of him. They even refused to believe that he was a disciple. Then Barnabas took him in charge and introduced him to the apostles. He explained to them how on his journey Saul had seen the Lord, who conversed with him and how Saul had been speaking fearlessly in the name of Jesus at Damascus [Acts 9:26–28].

Paul's teaching, however, stirred up so much trouble in Jerusalem that the community feared for his life and sent him back to Tarsus (Acts 9:29–30). Perhaps he was too controversial a figure and the Jerusalem Christians thought it best not to stir up another persecution. Years later, when the first community of Christians had been formed at Antioch, the church at Jerusalem sent Barnabas up to guide the new community. Barnabas remembered Paul and took the pains to travel all the way to Tarsus to ask him to join him in this new challenge (Acts 11:25).

For a whole year they worked together and "instructed large numbers" (Acts 11:26). It was an invaluable experience for Paul. He had the opportunity of witnessing how Jewish and Gentile Christians could live together in the new faith. He also received a firmer foundation in the Jerusalem catechesis which Barnabas knew so well. When the church at Antioch decided to send out their own "apostles," it was Baranabas and Paul who led the way. Barnabas had been a leader of the Antioch community (Acts 13:1, where he is named first, and Paul last!). He naturally took the leadership in the first expedition. However, great man that he was, Barnabas quickly realized Paul's special talents in this type of work and left the leadership in Paul's hands. After their success at Cyprus, Luke names Paul first: "From Paphos, Paul and his companions put out to sea and sailed to Pamphylia" (Acts 13:13).

Paul always remembered how much this training under Barnabas meant to him, and he tried to give others the same opportunity. He knew how much it meant to have a friend and companion to help him. Unfortunately we lack the details necessary to give a complete picture of the training he would give to others. We do know for example that at Lystra he selected a young man called Timothy, "since the brothers in Lystra and Iconium spoke highly of him" (Acts 16:2). We could not say that Timothy was a great success in his early years at work, if we examine only the data in Paul's letters. Paul himself may have had some doubts about his youth and inexperience when he sent him to Corinth, for he had to recommend him in a strong way:

> If Timothy should come to you, be sure to put him at ease among you. He does the Lord's work just as I do. So let no one treat him disdainfully!
> [1 Cor. 16:10–11]

Paul's misgivings were correct. Timothy was not equal to the situation at Corinth; at least we can infer this from the fact that Paul could not send him there again. It is Titus instead who figures prominently in the second epistle to the Corinthians and acts as messenger and ambassador. Paul however was patient with Timothy and knew that he had to learn through experience. There is reason to believe that he did gradually improve his leadership qualities, for later on Paul sends him on a mission to Philippi and speaks very highly of his qualities. He writes, "You know from experience what Timothy's qualities are, how he was like a son at his father's side serving the gospel along with me" (Phil. 2:22).

The training of co-workers for the apostolate was a slow process, and Paul realized that only by actual experience could a person develop the qualities needed for the rugged life of an apostle. Paul gave people the chance to do this under his direction, and so paved the way for the future by taking pains to form new leaders.

Local Apostolic Teamwork

When Paul approached a new community, his first concern was to obtain active collaborators, not passive recipients. As a result, we find him always associated with a group of local leaders and co-workers. The spread of the gospel had to be a joint effort, a local responsibility. Here again we do not have a detailed account of Paul's procedure, but we do have enough notable examples to get a good picture of his approach. Paul did not just help others, but he helped them to help others in turn.

At Corinth, he stayed at the home of a married couple whose names were Aquila and Priscilla. Their home became a meeting place of newly converted Christians. Their help was so valuable to Paul that when he left for Ephesus to begin the church there he took the fervent couple with him. He had such confidence in them that he left them there alone while he proceeded to Jerusalem to repay a vow he had made.

On his return to Ephesus he found that his trust had borne great fruit. Aquila and Priscilla had made great progress. One of their prominent converts was Apollos, an eloquent Jewish preacher from Alexandria. When Aquila and Priscilla heard him speaking of John's baptism, they invited him to their house and carefully taught him "God's new way" (Acts 18:27) in greater detail, showing how John the Baptist had prepared the way for Jesus. It must have been a great encouragement to Paul to find that this dynamic couple had already laid the foundations of the church at Ephesus. It was from the house of Aquila and Priscilla that Paul wrote to the church of Ephesus: "Aquila and Priscilla together with the assembly that meets in their house send you cordial greetings in the Lord" (1 Cor. 16:19).

Chapter 16 of Romans is precious for the long list it furnishes of Paul's close collaborators, men and women not *for whom* Paul worked, but *with whom*. Probably this appendix of Romans was originally a letter of recommendation of a certain Phoebe (Rom. 16:2) that Paul wrote to one of his communities, perhaps to Ephesus. He especially notes about a certain number that they have "labored among you" or "labored in the Lord." "Greet Mary who has labored much among you" (Rom. 16:6). "Greet Tryphaena and Tryphosa who labor in the Lord" (Rom. 16:12). "Greet the beloved Persis who has labored much in the Lord" (Rom. 16:12). For Paul, "to labor" means to cooperate actively in the spreading of the church.

In writing to the church at Corinth, Paul makes special mention of a group with which he has worked very closely:

> You know that the household of Stephanas is the first-fruits of Achaia, and is devoted to the service of the saints. I urge you to serve under such men and under everyone who cooperates and toils with them [1 Cor. 16:15–16].

The picture of a devoted team of lay workers also fits the church at Philippi. He refers to a certain "Epaphroditus" as his "brother, co-worker, and comrade in arms" (Phil. 2:25). Epaphroditus had been sent by the community to assist Paul during his imprisonment, but it is likely that he had previously been associated with him in apostolic work.

It is here at Philippi that we find important indications that Paul especially valued the role of women as lay apostles in the spread and growth of the church. It was Lydia, the seller of purple, who first received the Word of God in Philippi. She converted her household as well and insisted on Paul's coming to stay at her house, which became a center for the new church (Acts 16:12–15). Writing to Philippi later on, Paul mentions two other women there who had done notable service in spreading the good news. Yet it appears that there was a little squabble between them, for Paul had to write,

> I plead with Evodia just as I do with Syntyche: Come to some mutual understanding in the Lord. Yes, and I ask you too, my dependable fellow worker, to go to their aid; they have struggled at my side in promoting the Gospel along with Clement and the others who have labored with me whose names are in the book of life [Phil. 4:2].

If we had more information, we would be sure to find that women played a surprisingly great part in the work of the gospel, but, as it is, we have only hints. When Aquila and Priscilla are named, it is usually Priscilla's name that is mentioned first (Acts 18:18; 18:26; Rom. 16:3). This gives us a hint that she was the more active of the pair. In Romans 16, Paul mentions some ten women by name. He recommends a certain Phoebe who was in the ministry of the church at Cenchrae and who had greatly assisted him (Rom. 16:1). Priscilla and Aquila are mentioned as having "risked their own necks" for him (Rom. 16:3). Both Mary and Persis "have greatly labored" (Rom. 16:6,10). Tryphaena and Tryphosa had "labored in the Lord" (Rom. 16:12).

The association of so many women as collaborators with Paul may strike us as not unusual. However, for his own time, it was quite an innovation. Most people, in view of the position of women in ancient times, saw the role of women as essentially that of the housewife and mother devoted to serving the men and the children.

To sum up: Paul the apostle was essentially a team worker. His roving little community of apostles was at once a training school, a miniature church, and a mutual source of growth and support in a very difficult vocation. The same spirit was characteristic in his approach to new communities. His concern was always to invite others to work with him so that the growth of the church would be a joint responsibility and a joint effort.

Suggestions for Modern Christians

Teamwork in the apostolate is just as essential, if not more so, today. While each person has the gift of the Spirit, there is a certain fullness of the Spirit in a small group or community that is not present in the individual. In regard to presenting the church as a covenant community in Christ, can apostles effectively preach this and show it to the people unless they have actually experienced it themselves? Would it not be better if the people actually *saw* what they were trying to preach in the close-knit fellowship of a group of apostolic men and women?

In this modern age of specialization such an approach is becoming more and more necessary. The strongest influence on many people today no longer comes from the area where they live. The most important influence may be through an association at work, a recreational group, through various means of mass media such as radio, television, or newspaper. Hence the need of some specialization in knowing how to approach people from various angles according to the source of influence on their lives. One person alone could not hope effectively to use or even to get to know something of these vast fields of influence in the world today. However, when there is a community of apostolic workers all have some field of specialization of their own. This would be a great service to the whole group, as all pool their knowledge and skill to help the common task.

The team approach likewise becomes essential in modern times when we now realize that we must strive to develop a new type of leadership. We can no longer content ourselves with developing leaders only in the religious sphere. We must help to develop lay leaders within the particular tasks in the world to which they are called. These would be real *community* leaders who command the respect of the world. This calls for a much wider approach than centuries ago. It calls for a larger team of men and women, clergy and lay people who can pool together their resources from any special fields in order to help develop community leaders who will be real centers of influence.

5

The Apostle of Christ

The word "apostle" literally means "one sent." Christ himself loved to repeat continually that he was "one sent" from the Father. In the Gospel of John alone, the verb "send" is used over one hundred times. Jesus is the embodiment of God's love and power on earth. He is the one sent by God as his full representative. Yet this privilege was not to remain his alone. Jesus wanted to transfer all that the Spirit had given him to others as well. That is why the first message of the risen Christ to the assembled disciples was the words, "as the Father has sent me, so I send you" (John 20:21). Then to show that this was a complete transfer of what he had to others, he breathed on them and said, "receive the Holy Spirit." The disciples, through the Spirit, were to duplicate and continue Jesus' own work on earth. Thus every Christian, in this general sense, is an apostle—one sent by God through Jesus himself with the full gift of the Spirit.

However, in addition, some people in the early church as well as now have the additional vocation and gift of the Spirit that is called "apostle." This is a person whose main calling is to travel from place to place and make new foundations by starting Christian communities in places where Christ is not known, or very little known. Paul summarizes the meaning of this gift in his own life in Romans 15:18–21:

I will not dare to speak of anything except what Christ has done through me to win the Gentiles to obedience by word and deed, with mighty signs and marvels, by the power of God's Spirit. As a result, I have completed preaching the gospel of Christ from Jerusalem all the way around to Illyria. It has been a point of honor with me never to preach in places where Christ's name was already known, for I did not want to build on a foundation laid by another but rather to fulfill the words of Scripture, "They who received no word of him will see him, and they who have never heard will understand."

Looking at this description, we can single out several elements: (1) He directed his work particularly to the non-Jewish world, "to win the Gentiles to obedience." (2) His special work was that of a founder, to start communities in places where Christianity already existed: "It has been a point of honor with me never to preach in places where Christ's name was already known." (3) His plan was to make a circle of the main area of the Roman world, filling in where others had not gone: "I have completed preaching the gospel of Christ from Jerusalem all the way around to Illyria." He had already completed half the circuit, starting from Jerusalem going through Asia Minor and Southern Europe as far as the Adriatic Sea. The lower part of the circuit through Africa had already been completed by others. Now, starting from Rome he intended to complete the circle of the Roman world by going to Spain (Rom. 16:28). (4) His lifetime goal was to present to God as an offering priest the gift of the evangelization of the Gentile world: "To be a minister of Christ." The word "minister" in Greek is *leiturgos,* literally, a temple priest. His offering is one of people who have been evangelized: "that the Gentiles may be offered up as a pleasing sacrifice" (Rom. 16:16). Not that everyone in the area had been converted, but Paul wished to present the first-fruits of a great harvest of converts who would come as a result of the zeal and growth of the centers he had founded in strategic places.

A further indication of the meaning of "apostle" is found in his epistle to the Corinthians. He states emphatically, "Christ did not send me to baptize, but to preach the gospel" (1 Cor. 1:17), as if to say that the administration of the sacrament of initiation should be the responsibility of the community and its appointed leaders who would continue on after Paul left. His work was to "preach the gospel"—to initiate Christian communities in new localities. To be interpreted along the same lines is the comparison between himself and Apollos in 1 Cor. 3:5–11. He writes, "Thanks to the favor God showed me, I laid a foundation, as a wise master-builder, and now someone else is building upon it" (1 Cor. 3:10). His part then is to start the building of God, the Christian community, while others would build on that foundation.

Paul gives us another hint about the meaning of the vocation of an apostle in Colossians 1:21–29. After speaking of the "hope of the gospel" that they have received (1:23), he adds,

> It is the gospel which has been announced to every creature under heaven; and I, Paul, am its servant. Even now I find joy in the sufferings I endure for you. In my flesh I fill up what is lacking in the sufferings of Christ; for the sake of the church. I became a minister of this church through the commission God gave me to preach among you his word in its fullness—that mystery hidden for ages and generations past, but now revealed to his holy ones. God has willed to make known to them the glory beyond price which this mystery brings to the Gentiles—the mystery of Christ in you, your hope of glory! [Col. 1:23–28].

The emphasis throughout is on the preaching of the gospel: "the hope of the *gospel*"; "it has been announced to every creature under heaven" (Col. 1:23). This points to the preaching of the gospel in many new localities. He is concerned to make known what "this mystery brings to the *Gentiles*," which shows that he is especially dedicated to the non-Jewish world.

The completion of what is lacking in the sufferings of Christ can now be understood in view of his mission as an apostle. Wherever Christ goes, speaking through the apostle, there is always division among people; some accept the Word with joy while others reply with hostility and persecution. As a result, there is always new suffering on the part of Paul and the new members of Christ in every new locality where the gospel is preached. These are the "apostolic sufferings" that are connected with the preaching of the gospel. These must be completed by the new preaching of the gospel in place after place where Christ has not been heard before.

This interpretation is confirmed by Paul's frequent mention of the suffering and persecution that accompany the preaching of the gospel in new localities. He speaks of the "humiliation we had suffered at Philippi" (1 Thess. 2:2). He writes of his experience at Thessalonica: "You in turn became imitators of us and of the Lord, receiving the word despite great trials, with the joy that comes from the Holy Spirit . . ."(1 Thess. 1:6). In Second Corinthians he tells his people what characterizes "God's ministers": trials, difficulties, distresses, beatings, imprisonments, and riots (2 Cor. 6:6–10). In 2 Cor. 11:23, he asks if his opponents have the marks of an apostle of Christ; he writes, "are they ministers of Christ? Now I am really talking like a fool—I am more; in many more labors and imprisonments, with far worse beatings and frequent brushes with death."

Paul and the Twelve Apostles

What was Paul's relationship to the Twelve? First of all he notes that his vocation stands on a level with theirs; he came to know Christ through a direct appearance of the risen Christ just as they did. He writes, "Have I not seen Jesus our Lord?" (1 Cor. 9:1).

In regard to the Twelve, it is only Luke who consistently refers to them as "the apostles." What is primary is that they constituted the Twelve, the first witness of the risen Christ. In another sense they were more specifically "apostles" in that they went from place to place establishing new foundations. In the early church the vocation of "apostle" in this latter sense was a vocation that others besides Paul and the Twelve were called to. Paul considers Barnabas and others who worked with him as "apostles" (Cf. Gal. 2:9; 1 Thess. 2:6; Acts 14:13). So we can use the word "apostle" in three different senses: (1) someone who has had a direct call to bear official witness through an appearance of the risen Christ—this was limited to the Twelve, Paul, James, the brother of the Lord, and possibly some few others; (2) a general sense referring to all Christians who are "sent" by Christ to bear witness to his resurrection; (3) those who have received the call to devote full time service to the church through going from place to place establishing new communities. This last is the gift or charism of an apostle which many had both in the first century and in the later history of the church.

Paul gives us a valuable comparison between his own work and that of the Twelve in Galatians 2:7–9:

> On the contrary, recognizing that I had been entrusted with the gospel for the uncircumcised (for he who worked in Peter as an apostle among the Jews had been at work in me for the Gentiles), and recognizing, too, the favor bestowed on me, those who were the acknowledged pillars, James, Cephas, and John, gave Barnabas and me the handclasp of fellowship, signifying that we should go to the Gentiles, as they to the Jews.

Here we see that Peter, James, and John considered themselves as having an apostolate first of all to the Jews. They were apostles sent by Jesus to be witnesses of his Word among their Jewish brethren. They believed at first that the conversion of Israel had to come before the entry of the Gentiles into the church. Yet they recognized that the same Jesus who was working in them to accomplish this apostolate was also working in Paul to make him a witness to the Gentile world. They confirmed this by an agreement: by giving the "right hand of fellowship" to Paul. It is to be noted that Barnabas also had the same gift as Paul: "They gave to Barnabas and me the handclasp of fellowship, that we should go to the Gentiles." We can conclude from the text in Galatians that the Twelve were entrusted by the risen Christ with the vocation of establishing the church in new foundations through the Jewish world, whereas Paul considered that the same Christ had chosen him to accomplish the same task in traveling about the Gentile world.

The Vocation of Apostle
in Relationship to the Church

Paul notes the vocation of apostle in two separate lists of the various gifts or callings within the church. First in 1 Cor. 12:27–31:

> You, then, are the body of Christ. Every one of you is a member of it. Furthermore, God has set up in the church, first apostles, second prophets, third teachers, then miracle workers, healers, assistants, administrators, and those who speak in tongues.

The second list is in Ephesians 4:11–12:

> It is he who gave apostles, prophets, evangelists,

pastors, and teachers in roles of service to build
up the body of Christ.

In both lists the apostle has first mention. The apostles
are the ones who make the difficult beginnings; they
establish the community, hand it over to local leaders,
and then move on to start all over again with new hard-
ships. Yet all must do their part; all have their gifts for
"building up the body of Christ." The community de-
pends on the apostles for the beginning; they in turn
depend on many others in the community to help it
progress, grow, and stand on its own two feet as an
independent witness of Christ.

What has all this to do with Paul's "methods"? First,
we must say that Paul realized that all Christians had
their gifts or grace from the Spirit of the risen Jesus. The
contribution of all was needed in order to build the body
of Christ. Paul realized that he had one part, a most
important part, that of a founder. He concentrated on his
own particular role and never departed from it.

As for the part of others, he trusted in the Holy Spirit
working in other people according to their particular
gifts. He was confident that the Holy Spirit would work
in others to ensure good local leadership as well as the
growth and spread of the church. He knew that the Holy
Spirit, the totality of God's gift in Jesus, was in the whole
community, making it a vital organism and giving each
person a unique part to play in that organism. He was
sure that all the gifts of the Spirit could never be concentrated in any one person. God had willed to distribute
them among the members so they might learn to help
one another. God wished to teach them that no human
person could ever completely reflect God; all persons,
according to their gifts, must be instruments of the Holy
Spirit in some unique way that would be reinforced and
completed by many others.

Second, Paul was well aware that the preaching of the
good news in any place brought division among people.

Some would respond with their whole hearts; others would become bitter enemies. As in the experience of the prophets, only a "remnant," a part, would respond. Hence it was important for the whole work of Christ that there be certain ones who would go from place to place giving people the opportunity to form this "remnant" in as many places as possible. This nucleus could then be a light to those about them and gradually draw them to the faith. He considered it his responsibility to scatter the seed of the Word of God in as many different fields of the world as possible so that wherever it sprung up, it would gradually spread to the areas close by. He felt that growth was an essential element in the church. Each local community must take upon itself the responsibility of bringing the good news to those who were about them. The effect would be like that of leaven scattered in many parts of the dough so that each particle might more quickly and efficiently do its part in permeating the whole mass.

To sum up: In his letters, Paul shows that he was convinced that he had one very important role in the body of Christ: to be a traveling apostle, a man commissioned to preach and establish new foundations wherever the gospel had not yet come. His great success as a missioner was due to his confidence in Christ to work through him in this role and his whole-hearted dedication and concentration on his particular task. He also trusted that once he had done his part, the Holy Spirit would work in others to build the Christian community. These others would work on his foundation, strengthen and complete it so that it could be a perfect organism of the Holy Spirit *without Paul.*

Applications for Modern Christians

The serious situation in the world today demands a new concentration on the specific vocation of apostle— that is, men and women especially called and trained for the work of making new beginnings in non-Christian or dechristianized areas. There are many areas where native churches have been as much as twenty, fifty, or even a hundred years completely dependent on foreign clergy. The growing national consciousness of many of these areas makes this situation all the more perilous. On the other hand, parts of many "Christian" countries have a purely cultural Christianity that makes them really non-Christian from the viewpoint of real faith.

Taking a cue from Paul, the church needs men and women consecrated, devoted, and especially trained for the specific vocation of apostle. Today more than ever, this demands a most thorough preparation. Apostles must devote themselves to a thorough study of the world they live in: languages, literature, cultures, and values, using the best methods that science can provide. Apostles will be well trained in theology, able to communicate effectively the basic truths of their faith in terms understandable in the world and culture where they live. They will concentrate on their particular role in the church, leaving the follow-up to others. Their vocation will be essentially one of service to a new community in its efforts to become a complete, self-sufficient organism of the Holy Spirit. Needless to say, they will be especially adept at making new friends in new places; they will be able to get others to work with them in such a way that they will see the work and responsibility of the Christian community as their own.

As with Paul, such people must be endowed with an unusual trust in the Holy Spirit working in others. This spirit of confidence will inspire a true and lasting community development in Christ. Since the particular task of the apostles is to initiate, they will consider it their duty to be continually preparing the community for their withdrawal. They will feel they have done their greatest service to the community when they have become no longer needed and are free to start all over in another place.

It is easy to see that the vocation of apostle is an un-

usual one. However, numbers are not nearly as important as quality and preparation for this task. The work of
the apostle, if well done, will lay the groundwork for
unlimited numbers to enter the church. Apostles will not
measure success by the large numbers that are brought to
Christ. The only criterion will be a community strong
enough not only to exist by itself but grow indefinitely
through its careful work in developing local leaders.

In regard to many so-called "Christian areas," the
church must once again become apostolic and train its
ministers to be primarily apostles. Many Christian communities have a stifling atmosphere of passivity because
the clergy have assumed or controlled most of the gifts of
the Spirit that Paul saw as spread through the community. The clergy and ordained ministers must concentrate
on the gift of the apostle and trust the Holy Spirit to
develop every other kind of local leadership and gift
needed by the community. The work of the minister or
priest must be viewed as primarily apostolic: helping to
create Christians and making no presumptions that people are such merely because of their presence in church
gatherings.

However, it must not be assumed that Paul's special
gift of the apostle is to be limited to clergy, religious, and
special ministers. As we have seen, Paul refused to concentrate on work that today we would usually associate
only with ministers and priests. He wrote to the Corinthians, "Christ did not send me to baptize, but to preach
the gospel" (1 Cor. 1:17). Christians carry the role of
traveling apostle every time they travel to a new place or
meet a stranger. The sign of God's unconditional love is
manifest in the special attention we show to people we
have never met before, and may never meet again. It has
very specific application to tourists and visitors to foreign
countries. Visitors are not merely sight-seers but ambas-
sadors of their own country and of the faith and convictions they live by. This faith prompts them to love and
respect the language, culture, and customs of others to

such an extent that they take pains to learn what they can about them before and while visiting them. When this happens, the millions of tourists who flow from one country and place to another can be living representatives of the oneness of God they believe in. As such, they will create oneness, community, and the beginnings of Christian faith wherever they go.

6

Teacher of Teachers

Paul himself is the most valuable source of information we have on "teaching methods" in the early church. It was his special policy (Rom. 15:20) never to go where there was already an established Christian church. Consequently, he himself taught the first Christian converts. When it came to instructing other converts, after Paul's departure, no doubt they followed Paul's approach to teaching. Fortunately, we have considerable information about his teaching approach.

The first letter to the Thessalonians, written about A.D. 49 or 50, may be the earliest Christian document that we possess. Here Paul definitely states that the first Christians learned their new way of life by imitating the "little church" composed of Paul and his companions. He wrote, "Now, my brothers, we beg and exhort you, in the Lord Jesus, that even as you have learned from us how to conduct yourselves in a way pleasing to God . . . so you must learn to make more and more progress" (1 Thess. 4:1). He appealed to their memory of the lifestyle of the apostolic team: "You know as well as we do what we proved to be like when, while still among you, we acted on your behalf. You in turn became imitators of us and the Lord" (1 Thess. 1:5–6).

This imitation was not merely in general terms; we find specific ways they did this as we read through the letter. For example, Paul and his companions worked day and night with their own hands (1 Thess. 2:9) in order to win the respect of outsiders. He reminds the Thessalonians to likewise work hard so they will give a good example to those outside the community (1 Thess. 4:11–12). Personal attention and individual encouragement were characteristic of the apostles: "You likewise know how we exhorted every one of you as a father does his children—How we encouraged you . . . to make your lives worthy of God . . . " (1 Thess. 2:11). In the same manner, he instructed the converts to encourage one another and build up one another (1 Thess. 4:18; 5:11).

The letters to the Corinthians make their strongest arguments through an appeal to Paul's example as a teacher. In First Corinthians he writes, "I became your father in Christ Jesus through the gospel. I beg you, then, become imitators of me" (1 Cor. 4:16). Again, "Imitate me as I imitate Christ" (1 Cor. 11:1). This verse is of special interest because it shows that imitation of Christ does not mean some abstract example or memory of the past, but an *imitation of the life of Christ as exemplified in Paul.* Later we will show the implications of this for Paul's concept of apostolic tradition.

Specific examples of this imitation are found throughout his letter. Divisions have sprung up in the community with little groups gathering around their favorite teachers and often judging each other (1 Cor. 1:10–17). However, Paul refuses to judge his fellow teachers; this is God's work (1 Cor. 3:5–15). He is one at heart with Apollos, one of the favorite Corinthian teachers. Their unity should be an example for the Corinthians as well: "Brothers, I have applied all this to myself and Apollos by way of example for your benefit. May you learn by us . . . " (1 Cor. 4:6).

In other matters, also, Paul carefully points out his own practice as a model for Christians. The new converts at Corinth preferred the showy, individual ecstatic gifts of the Spirit such as tongues (1 Cor. 12–14). Paul states that he himself possessed this gift (1 Cor. 14:18), yet for their benefit he preferred not to use it in public gatherings but to teach and prophesy (1 Cor. 14:6, 19). In addition, when he states that the celibate life is preferable in view of the imminence of the kingdom, his own life as a celibate stands behind his words (1 Cor.7:6–7). A great cause of division in the community was the question of eating meats that had at some time been sacrificed to idols but were now sold in the market or in a restaurant. Paul affirms the principle of freedom of conscience, yet states that this freedom should never be the cause of another's downfall (1 Cor. 8:11–12). In his own life, he would rather never eat meat than cause another to fall (1 Cor. 8:13).

On reading Second Corinthians, we can see that Paul was rather reluctant to communicate through letters. He deeply regrets that he was not able to visit them again as he had planned (2 Cor. 1:15). In fact, he does not rely on letters, as others do who put their trust in impressive letters of recommendation. His "letter" is the community itself, which he has so formed as a living print of its founder:

> You are my letter, known and read by all men, written on your hearts. Clearly you are a letter of Christ which I have delivered, a letter written not with ink but by the Spirit of the living God, not on tablets of stone but on tablets of flesh in the heart [2 Cor. 3:2–3].

These verses, filled with such deep feeling, tell us to what extent Paul considered the community to be modeled on the lives of the apostles who founded it.

Paul's own criterion for a true apostle is of special interest: It is a manner of life completely dedicated to others even when this entails intense suffering and heroic personal sacrifice. He writes, "we do all we can to present ourselves as ministers of God . . ." (2 Cor. 6:4). Among what he undergoes are trials, difficulties, distresses, beatings, imprisonments, riots, hard work, sleepless nights, and fastings (2 Cor. 6:4–5). These are the actual proofs that he has been sent by Christ, the criteria of an apostle. This is the way he teaches people what it means to be a Christian.

There is a specific very personal reference to imitation in this letter. Someone had made a very serious attack on Paul, prompting him to write a letter in sorrow and tears (2 Cor. 2:2–4). In this letter he had asked the community to take action against the offender. Now, however, he writes them to forgive the man just as he himself has forgiven him, despite the severe injury to his reputation: "If you forgive a man anything, so do I. Any forgiving I have done has been for your sakes, and before Christ" (2 Cor. 2:10).

Paul's fiery letter to the Galatians has often been called the gospel of Christian freedom. Paul has to defend the gospel of Christ against those who were claiming that the good news required a person to be also a Jew in the sense of adherence to many of the observances of the Mosaic Law. This would make it practically impossible to gain Gentile converts. It would also make Jew-Gentile fellowship virtually nonexistent if the Jewish food regulations were strictly observed. Paul begs the community to follow his example in this matter. He writes, "I beg you, brothers, to become like me, as I became like you" (Gal. 4:12). He illustrates this with the powerful imitation image of the child-parent relationship: "You are my children, and you put me back in labor pains until Christ is formed in you" (Gal. 4:19).

Once again, Paul's great appeal is to his own example. He above all was a Jew of Jews, a perfect observer of the Law, a fanatic persecutor of the church of God (Gal. 1:13–14). His own conversion was a great act of God's grace, and he has never gone back to the Law despite persecution and great difficulties. He even had to go as far as to rebuke Peter himself for compromising the gospel in order to preserve the Law.

This confrontation with Peter took place when Peter visited Antioch. At first he freely ate with the Gentiles, despite the Jewish dietary laws. However, when other Jews came up to Antioch from Jerusalem, he refused to eat with the Gentiles, and ate only with his fellow Jewish Christians. In effect, this was saying in action that the Gentiles were second-class citizens who needed something more in order to be perfect Christians. Paul directly withstood him (Gal. 2:11). In front of the whole assembly he called Peter to task for not living the truth of the gospel in practice (Gal. 2:14).

The letter to the Galatians ends with a powerful thrust at Paul's enemies. They may glory in other marks on their bodies (the circumcision) but he will glory only in the marks, *stigmata*, of the Lord Jesus. These marks are the visible testimony of his sufferings: They are the lash-marks on his body as the direct result of persecution for the truth of the gospel. Thus they identify him with Christ himself who suffered in the same way.

Philippi, Paul's first church in Europe, was his favorite community. They were so faithful to him that they supported him in his work wherever he went. They did this by sending letters, gifts, and even personal service when he was in prison. So we would expect this to be his most intimate letter. It is here that he makes the strongest appeal to the manner of life they learned by imitating him when he first taught them. He writes, "Become imitators of me, my brothers. Take as your guide those who follow the example we have set" (Phil. 3:17). He recalls their first learning experience in these words, "Live according to what you have learned and accepted, what you have heard me say and seen me do" (Phil. 4:9).

He applies this especially to those who were tempted to look back to their past practices in Judaism. He himself was a circumcised Jew, a Hebrew of Hebrews, a fervent Pharisee, and a persecutor of the church (Phil. 3:5–6). He regards this "brilliant" past as refuse and garbage now that he has found Christ (Phil. 3:8). Like a marathon runner, he never looks back but ahead to the finish line, the prize of life in Christ (Phil. 3:13–14).

A delightful final touch to the theme of imitation is found in Paul's little letter to Philemon. Philemon was a well-to-do convert of Paul whose home became an important church center where Paul had stayed many times. A slave of Philemon had run away, robbed his master, and had come to Paul who was in prison. Paul instructed him and baptized him. The slave stayed for a time near Paul in prison in order to care for his needs. Finally, the Apostle sent him home with a message to his former master asking for forgiveness, acceptance as a brother, and even his freedom.

Of special interest is the way Paul regards the slave once he has instructed him. He is "my child, whom I have begotten during my imprisonment" (Philem. 10). In sending him back to his master he is really sending back his very heart (Philem. 12). Hence Philemon should receive him as Paul himself (Philem. 17). This illustrates the degree that the disciple becomes like the teacher. Since as a Christian he has now become truly a brother to Paul, the Apostle asks his master to receive him no longer as a slave but as a beloved brother. As a brother, Paul agrees to pay back any money the slave owes his master. Paul is confident that Philemon will do even more than he asks (Philem. 21). This may be hinting that he grant the slave freedom. Throughout the letter, Paul asks nothing of Philemon that he has not first done himself by way of example.

Paul and Apostolic Tradition

Paul's insistence on imitation may strike modern readers as quite egotistical, if we do not understand the Apostle's motives. He speaks in this way only to churches he himself has founded. As a founder, he has brought to them a living tradition, an *apostolic tradition* that goes back to Jesus himself. His own life has been a necessary mediating link between Jesus and the new churches. Since this point is so important, we will illustrate it with pertinent texts from his letters. Here we must present again some texts we have already studied, but we will examine them from a new viewpoint.

Paul is not interested in any kind of slavish or mechanical imitation of his own life: In writing to the Thessalonians he stated, "You in turn became imitators of us and *of the Lord,* receiving the word despite great trials . . ." (1 Thess. 1:6). The persecution that Paul undergoes is really that of Jesus himself. It is this particular aspect that Christians are to imitate when they are harassed because of their faith.

The Apostle carries this thought further by writing, "Brothers, you have been made like the churches of God in Judea which are in Christ Jesus" (1 Thess. 2:14). These first churches were probably those formed by the seven Greek assistants of the Twelve (Acts 6). They bore the special brunt of the first persecution of the early church. They became a pattern for the larger church because of their very close solidarity with Jesus himself who suffered in the same way: "You suffer the same treatment from your fellow countrymen as they did from the Jews who killed the Lord Jesus and the prophets . . ." (1 Thess. 2:15).

Paul makes a very strong appeal to his *apostolic authority* in 2 Thess. 3:6–9:

> We command you, brothers, in the name of the Lord Jesus Christ to avoid any brother who wanders from the straight path and does not follow the tradition you received from us. You know how you ought to imitate us.

Paul then goes on to describe the manner of his life, in particular his hard work in self-support in order to avoid imposing on anyone. He did this for them as an example to imitate (2 Thess. 3:9). The solemn injunction in the

name of the Lord Jesus Christ shows the authority behind his statement. Yet it is not an authority based on the
power of dominion, but rather on a life that is led in
conformity with the gospel. Paul has been the founder of
the community. Thus he has come to them as Christ
himself. As a consequence, since his own life is the direct
link with Christ, he can present himself as a concrete
example of Christian tradition that is to be handed on to
others. *This is his apostolic authority.*

In 1 Corinthians, Paul faces opponents who make a
claim to apostolic authority through letters of recommendation or association with prominent church leaders
in Judea. He counters this by presenting the criteria for a
true apostle. When he writes "apostle," it is in the literal
sense of one sent by Christ to act on his behalf. It is a
traveling founder of new churches who has gone
through the same experience of hardship and suffering
as Jesus himself. Paul wants to be regarded as a "servant
of Christ" and "administrator of God's mysteries" (1
Cor. 4:1). Then he points out how this can be verified:
"Up to this very hour we go hungry and thirsty, poorly
clad, roughly treated, wandering about homeless."

It is only because he has fulfilled these criteria and has
been their father through the preaching of the gospel (1
Cor. 4:15) that he can say, "Be imitators of me" (1 Cor.
4:16). At this time Paul cannot actually be present to
furnish them that example, so he sends Timothy, his
"other-self" as a "beloved and faithful son" (1 Cor. 4:17)
to remind them of his "ways in Christ." When Paul asks
for imitation, it is only that they follow him in his own
imitation of Christ: "Be imitators of me, as I am of Christ"
(1 Cor. 11:1).

Paul does not use such imitation formulas in writing to
churches that he himself has not founded. Instead, he
uses general terms that refer to doing things as Christ did
(Rom. 15:7; Col. 3:13). In view of this, and the texts cited
above, we can state with a high degree of certainty that
imitation is based on the fact that a community has ac-

cepted the gospel of Christ from Paul. This gospel as preached by him, and lived by him, constitutes his own personal witness to Christ. Paul represents him and acts in his name by carrying on the same role and mission as a servant of God. His "apostolic authority" is an authentic embodiment of the gospel in his own life to such a degree that it can be a living Christian tradition that will be handed on to others.

To sum up, Paul's approach to teaching is especially valuable since he was a founder of new churches and set a pattern that others followed. Throughout his letters, he continually refers to his readers' vivid memory of his own lifestyle. It was this life in Christ that was to be their guide. Yet Paul is not interested in any mechanical imitation of himself. He is interested in *apostolic tradition*. This is imitation of Christ himself as mirrored in his own personal response to the gospel, since Paul has been the first living link between his converts and Christ.

Suggestions for the Modern Apostle

To use many words at this point would be to clutter up the simple lesson of Paul, teacher of many Christian teachers. The Spirit speaks to others not through words and concepts, but directly through human lives. When the Spirit truly lives in you and guides your life, you will find yourself with less and less actually to say because your own lifestyle will be the essential message.

7

A Gospel of Freedom
and Liberation

"You have been called to freedom!" (Gal. 5:13)

"It was for liberty that Christ freed us." (Gal. 5:1)

These were the vibrant, reassuring words that Paul spoke again and again to his disciples. One of the great reasons why Christianity spread like wildfire through the world in the first three centuries was precisely this—that it was a proclamation of freedom addressed to a world shackled by the bonds of compulsive religious worship and hemmed in by impenetrable walls of social, racial, and economic barriers.

First of all there were shackles imposed by the disheartening segregation between Jew and Greek, between slave and free, between man and woman. Because of Jewish dietary regulations, Jew and Greek could not eat together at the same table. The population of many Greek and Roman cities was almost 50 percent slaves, men and women who through no fault of their own led an existence characterized by fear and lack of human dignity. The woman before civil and religious law was not recognized as having the same rights as a man.

In view of this we can well understand the pointed

significance of the three great blessings pronounced in the Jewish synagogue in ancient times:

> Blessed be thou O Lord our God, . . .
> who has not made me a Gentile, . . .
> who has not made me a slave, . . .
> who has not made me a woman!

Paul had these great barriers in mind when he thought of the new unity of those baptized in Christ. He proclaimed,

> There does not exist among you Jew or Greek,
> slave or free man, male or female [Gal. 3:28].

The great center of unity was the Eucharistic table. Before the one Lord of all, master and slave, man and woman, Jew and Greek sat as equals and partook of the same holy bread. In view of their common union with Christ, the slave was a "freed man of the Lord" (1 Cor. 7:22); the Greek was no longer a "stranger and alien" to the promises made to Israel, but a "fellow citizen and member of God's household" (Eph. 2:19); the woman was no longer a mere subject of man because of her status, but loved and respected by her husband in the same way that Christ cherished the church (Eph. 5:25). This intimate union about the table of the Lord did not mean that deep-seated institutions were immediately transformed. It did however indicate that the seeds of change were being sown, a seed that would grow slowly but forcibly to bring about the transformation of social barriers. If a slave, for instance, must be respected as a "brother in the Lord" (Philem. 16), then slavery itself was doomed eventually to disappear.

In special reference to women, we must look at Paul's attitude in the light of his own times, where he would be regarded as quite radical. As a trained Jewish teacher, he well knew that no rabbi of his time accepted women disciples. Yet Paul broke away from this tradition because he was convinced that the gospel was truly meant to give women a new freedom and equality before God. When he proclaimed there is "no longer male and female" he was thinking of the baptismal ceremony where all were so united with Christ that they took on a new identity and new name, that of Jesus himself. This was symbolized by putting on a new white garment to signify the new person in Christ that they had become: "All of you who have been baptized into Christ have clothed yourselves with him" (Gal. 3:27). Following this statement, Paul notes that there is no longer male and female because these differences now appear to be insignificant in view of the new oneness between man and woman through the Spirit.

In his own apostolic practice, as we saw in Chapter 4, Paul did not adopt the common attitude that Christian women were to find their role only in devoted service within the home. Instead, he welcomed women as close collaborators and as people who took the initiative in spreading the gospel. The Acts of the Apostles makes special note of the prominent women disciples accepted by Paul (Acts 16:11–15; 17:4,12,33). Especially notable was the fact that the whole European apostolate began in Philippi in Greece, where the first converts were from an audience composed entirely of women who had gathered near the river for prayer. One of the women was called Lydia. Her household became an important church in Greece (Acts 16:13–15).

In writing to his Christians, Paul put in practice his own convictions about women's equality and liberation in Christ. In regard to the obligations of spouses, he is careful to address both men and women equally so the matter will be seen from both sides, not from the man's only:

> To avoid immorality, every man should have his own wife and every woman her own husband.

The husband should fulfill his conjugal obligations toward his wife, the wife hers toward her husband. A wife does not belong to herself but to her husband; equally, a husband does not belong to himself but to his wife [1 Cor. 7:3–4].

When Paul writes about Jesus' teaching on divorce, he carefully spells out the woman's obligation as well, even though divorce was usually a male prerogative in ancient times. In fact, he mentions the wife first: "A wife must not separate from her husband. If she does separate, she must either remain single or become reconciled to him again. Similarly, a husband must not divorce his wife" (1 Cor. 7:10–11). The same equal treatment is seen in the "Pauline Privilege." When there was a marriage in which either the woman or the man had become a convert, there should be every effort of the Christian spouse to win over the partner through love and example. If this does not succeed, then the Christian wife or husband is free from the bond of marriage in this circumstance (1 Cor. 7:13–16).

In regard to Paul and women, the famous passage about women's veils in 1 Corinthians 11 often makes people assume that Paul was biased against women. The situation in the Christian community at Corinth was that women were using their new-found freedom to stand up to pray and prophesy aloud with their heads unveiled during Christian worship. The fact that they dared to do this despite the force of custom and tradition is already an indication of the new freedom they felt as the result of Paul's teaching. However, a number of men and women of Corinth were not ready for this new liberation and wrote to Paul at Ephesus to complain about it. Paul's reply is an attempt to conciliate these differences and restore peace in the community. He does not silence the women. His particular point is against removal of women's veils, which he regards as an attempt merely to imitate men. Paul does not appear to be ready for the idea that women's new freedom in the gospel will change her whole status in society. In this case, it does not seem that Paul himself realized the full implications of the social message of the gospel.

The second slavery that the world of St. Paul faced was that of religious observances. Most people felt that there were certain things that "had to be done" in order to win the favor of the gods. To neglect to do so would be to court disaster at the hands of some offended god. The Romans, for example, felt that the sacrifices offered to the gods were necessary to preserve the empire from disaster. This attitude bred fear and a spirit of compulsion; there was always the possibility that something was left undone in the service of the gods. Paul describes the former condition of his converts in this slavery when he writes, "In the past, when you did not acknowledge God, you served as slaves to gods who are not really divine" (Gal. 4:8).

What a sigh of relief must have escaped from Paul's audiences when he promised them freedom from such slavery. He preached a God of love who asked no precondition, no gift, no previous work to earn his love. It was precisely in their actual condition of weak sinners that Christ loved them:

> At the appointed time, when we were still powerless, Christ died for us godless men. It is rare that anyone should lay down his life for a just man, though it is barely possible that for a good man someone may have the courage to die. It is precisely in this that God proves his love for us: that while we were still sinners, Christ died for us [Rom. 5:6–8].

This was the gospel of freedom and love that Paul preached—that a person did not have to do something first to earn God's love, but rather that God first loved us and would give us the strength to do all things if we surrender ourselves in faith to that love.

The third freedom that Paul proclaimed was similar to the one above. It was the freedom from the necessity of law, in the sense of an external, necessary, coercive guide that would be one's only hope of doing good and avoiding evil. What Paul proclaimed was the liberating intervention of a loving Person into human lives, the love of Christ which would transform them from within and give them an inner source of courage and assurance.

Consequently, Paul did not require his Gentile converts to follow any of the Old Testament biblical laws and observances. This was contrary to the usual requirements of Jewish and even some Christian missionaries. He asked of his converts nothing more than a simple response and surrender to the love of Christ that manifested itself in devoted service of one's neighbor. It was here that he left himself open to later attacks by Judaizers. They insisted that the regulations of the Old Testament such as circumcision were a necessary response for the Christian. Paul fought with all his might against such a supposition. If something in addition to Christ's love was necessary, then all that Christ did was not enough. In other words, it was in vain if something else were really needed. So Paul insisted to the Galatians:

> It was for liberty that Christ freed us. So stand firm, and do not take on yourselves the yoke of slavery a second time. Pay close attention to me, Paul, when I tell you that if you have yourselves circumcised, Christ will be of no use to you [Gal. 5:1–2].

Hence the only "law" or obligation a person faces is that which flows from union with a Father who loves his children. Joined to such a Father, we must love our brothers and sisters in that same love:

Owe no debt to anyone except the debt that binds us to love one another. He who loves his neighbor has fulfilled the Law [Rom. 13:8].

The final and greatest slavery from which a person could be freed was "the law of sin and death." This was the powerlessness of people to do the good they wished to do in their hearts, and the consequences of this weakness.

There is no condemnation for those who are in Christ Jesus. The Law of the Spirit, the Spirit of life in Christ Jesus has freed you from the law of sin and death [Rom. 8:1].

The "law of sin and death" was the inevitable human condition. Through weakness, people turned from God and could do nothing but await the consequence of their deeds, which would be a permanent death. But the gospel of the saving forgiveness of Jesus changed the condition of sinners from a liability into being the very object of God's compassion and mercy. This new friendship with God would be forever, and death would no longer separate a person from God.

When the corruptible frame takes on incorruptibility and the mortal immortality, then will the saying of Scripture be fulfilled, "Death is swallowed up in victory." O death, where is your victory? O death, where is your sting? Now the sting of death is sin, and sin gets its power from the Law. But thanks be to God who has given us the victory through our Lord Jesus Christ [1 Cor. 15:54–57].

But how to use all these new freedoms? Here Paul pointed to Jesus himself. How did Jesus use his power, glory, and freedom as a Son of God? Since a Christian became a child of God through receiving the Spirit of Jesus (Gal. 4:6), the way of Jesus must be the Christian's way also. The freedom of the Christian, the child of God, is to be used in the same way as that of Christ the Son of God. It is a freedom that prompts a willing and complete life of service to others. Freedom alone is not enough. With this in mind, Paul says to the Galatians, "You have been called to live in freedom—but not a freedom that gives rein to the flesh. Out of love place yourselves at one another's service" (Gal. 5:13).

As for Paul himself, his whole life was dedicated to this ideal, to preach Jesus as the Lord of freedom, and himself as the servant of others. "For it is not ourselves we preach, but Christ Jesus as Lord, and ourselves as your servants for Jesus' sake" (2 Cor. 4:5).

To sum up: Paul's gospel was a gospel of freedom. He saw the risen Christ as a truly liberating person who could deliver people from the terrible imprisonment affected by social and racial barriers. Paul presented the image of a God of love who would free men and women from the bonds of legalism and necessary religious observances. Above all he presented the risen Christ as the one who could free us from slavery to sin and fear of death. The new state of people bound to Christ was that of complete freedom, not from responsibility, but the liberty to devote all their energies to a real service of others prompted by love.

Applications for Modern Christians

Today, the world more than ever yearns for deliverance from any kind of servitude or oppression. The social unrest in many countries, the demands of minority groups for recognition and respect all point to this. This means that the message of the modern apostle must be one of radical freedom. In one way, the situation is more dangerous than in ancient times, for much that goes on is hidden and beneath the surface. Many laws, for example, protect minorities, whether religious, racial, or cultural. These laws of course must be strengthened and vigorously applied. Yet an outer courtesy sometimes covers up a subtle disdain for others that is more an occasion for suffering than anything else.

It is not enough to point out precepts of charity. Christ did not come on earth to give precepts but to show us how to love one another as brothers and sisters, and that not in name only but in affection and respect also. Modern apostles cannot be satisfied only by "demonstrations"; they can only point to the wound. Their demonstration must in addition be from within, to attack the root of the evil. Statements and sermons, however forceful, are good but not enough; action is required.

This type of action can manifest itself in many ways: cooperative action with religious leaders of other beliefs or secular organizations dedicated to just causes; familiar association with minority groups, whether racial or cultural. However, it is also important that Christians try to influence the actual offenders themselves rather than being content with condemnations. They must be ready to work with them on a personal basis, in small groups, trying to understand them and give them the support they need to face the deep fears that are causing them to withdraw from the possibility of encounter with some group of fellow human beings. This of course will take long, patient work over many years and will not make the headlines, but it is a truly Christ-like approach. It will effectively show that there is a gospel of freedom.

Today some of the great religions of antiquity are slowly losing ground. Their gods of fear no longer grasp modern people. However a certain "neo-paganism" is taking its place. The ancient gods offered a certain security to those who performed the necessary cult. Likewise today there are many who hold out the prospect of security in a full human life to those who make use of all that scientific progress affords in the way of material goods, and in a way of life based on the human wisdom provided by findings in philosophy, psychology, and other disciplines. Here it must be a question of good use, but not complete dependence; otherwise it is a new slavery and even sad frustration for those who through no fault of their own do not have these means at their disposition. The apostle today must search in any culture for the chains that take away anyone's freedom. These can be a starting point for preaching that only the liberty of the gospel offers us true independence and security. It is only in Christ Jesus that we can be freed from human dependence and be dependent only on a God who wants partners and co-workers rather than slaves.

When Paul preached the good news, it was the "newness" of the Christian faith that won such fervent adherents; all felt that they could break from the past and make a new start by an immediate response to a "young" risen Christ who was not bound by the past, nor by any age. The apostle of today must give people today the same opportunity that Paul gave his hearers. Christians themselves may have learned a response, a Law, through many years of work or study. However, to others they must preach a gospel, not a response, for it is only the Word that has the power to save, not the Law. Hence we must be careful to attach no human conditions to the gospel, so that people today can make the same fresh start the first hearers of Paul made.

At the same time we must avoid the trap of presenting a "gospel of liberation" that would be purely internal. This might be very appealing to a middle- or upper-class person quite satisfied with things as they are in the world as it is. We are very much indebted to Christians in the Third World for pointing out to us the true nature of a theology of liberation. It must necessarily affect and change injustice due to economic, social, or political oppression that prevents any person from enjoying true dignity and freedom and a just share of the material resources of the world. Paul was certainly a man of his times and probably was not ready himself for the full implications of the social message of the gospel. Yet even with his own limitations he was concerned that the message of Christ should mean not only a spiritual oneness but an equality in the social and economic order as well. This was the purpose behind the ecumenical collection that he took up all over the world for the poor in Jerusalem.

8

The Wisdom and
Folly of the Cross

The Approach of Paul:
Preaching and Living the Cross

A good example of Paul's attitude and approach is found in his apostolate to the city of Corinth. Corinth was a great metropolis of pleasure, business, religion, and culture in the ancient world. It was a port city, a meeting place between east and west. All trade shipping stopped there and brought cargos overland across the narrow isthmus of central Greece to the port of Cenchrae on the other side. This was much preferable to and much shorter than the long treacherous sea journey around Greece and thence to Rome. Corinth was so well known in the ancient world that the verb to "Corinthiaze" meant to "really live it up." The phrase "a Corinthian girl" was equivalent to a prostitute. The name "a Corinthian man" meant a sharp merchant or businessman. When Paul came to Corinth it was a real challenge to the gospel. What power did it have to really affect an urban center like this, one of the greatest cities of the Roman empire?

Most religion teachers or traveling philosophers of the day made every possible attempt to allure and attract audiences and disciples. There were numerous philosopher gurus of the day who walked around followed by their school of disciples who gloried in imitating their master and basking in his fame. It would have been easy for Paul to imitate this rather successful approach. In fact, when the Christian community started at Corinth, many believers, according to the Greek model, tried to attach themselves to various Christian teachers and prided themselves on the qualities of their masters:

> I have been informed, my brothers, by certain members of Chloe's household that you are quarreling among yourselves. This is what I mean: One of you will say, "I belong to Paul," another, "I belong to Apollos," still another, "Cephas has my allegiance . . . ," and the fourth, "I belong to Christ" [1 Cor. 1:11–12].

In contrast to the Greek wisdom teachers of the day, Paul's attitude and approach was one of complete trust in the cross, both in his personal life and in the message that he preached:

> As for myself, brothers, when I came to you, I did not come proclaiming God's testimony with any particular eloquence or "wisdom." No, I determined that while I was with you, I would speak of nothing but Jesus Christ and him crucified. When I came among you it was in weakness and fear, and with much trepidation. My message and my preaching had none of the persuasive force of "wise" argumentation, but the convincing power of the Spirit. As a consequence, your faith rests not on the wisdom of men but on the power of God [1 Cor. 2:1–5].

Paul's great concern was that any success would be due to God's power and not mere human plans or achievement. In preaching the cross, he was going diametrically opposite to everything that the Greeks looked forward to. With their love of philosophy, they wanted a beautiful and appealing knowledge that would satisfy their desire to penetrate deeply into the mysteries of the cosmos. Instead, Paul spoke about a man who had died a disgraceful criminal death on the cross. His purpose was to turn them away from the quest for sages and gurus who could show them the way through a human system of thought. "Where is the wise man to be found? Where the scribe? Where is the master of worldly argument? Has not God turned the wisdom of this world into folly?" (1 Cor. 1:20). To confound the human search for outside masters or teachers, God had chosen to save people through the folly of the cross. "Since in God's wisdom the world did not come to know him through 'wisdom,' it pleased God to save those who believe through the absurdity of the preaching of the gospel" (1 Cor. 1:21).

In a beautiful passage, Paul shows how opposed the preaching of the cross was to both Greek and Jewish expectations. To the latter, it was opposed because of national, political, and messianic hopes that were built on the idea of power and triumph over their enemies. This would begin through a great sign from heaven:

> Yes, Jews demand "signs" and Greeks look for "wisdom," but we preach Christ crucified—a stumbling block to Jews, and an absurdity to Gentiles; but to those who are called, Jews and Greeks alike, Christ the power of God and the wisdom of God. For God's folly is wiser than men, and his weakness more powerful than men [1 Cor. 1:22–25].

In view of this conviction, Paul did not begin his apostolate in Corinth by appealing to the more educated and influential people who could have won him a hearing with others. He chose, like Christ himself, to go to the poor, the weak, the slaves, the oppressed, those least likely to impress others. This would have the effect of shaming the strong and wise. No one could boast of any human achievement. It would be a pure sign of God's intervention.

> Consider your situation. Not many of you are wise, as men account wisdom; not many are influential; and surely not many are wellborn. God chose those whom the world considers absurd to shame the wise; he singled out the weak of this world to shame the strong. He chose the world's lowborn and despised, those who count for nothing to reduce to nothing those who were something; so that mankind can do no boasting before God [1 Cor. 1:26–29].

As a result, there is an entirely new wisdom available to people. It is the wisdom of God himself shown in Christ Jesus through the folly of the cross: "God has made him our wisdom and also our justice, our sanctification, and our redemption. This is just as you find it written, 'Let him who would boast, boast in the Lord' " (1 Cor. 1:30–31). Since this new wisdom is entirely independent of the world and its usual standards, it provides a whole new insight into a deeper reality than the world can possibly know. It furnishes a unique standard of life that is able to judge the world because it is independent of it and of any teachers that the world can furnish. It is a wisdom that goes far beyond whatever the human senses can reach to: "Eye has not seen, ear has not heard, nor has it so much as dawned on man what God has prepared for those who love him" (1 Cor. 2:9).

It is a complete gift of God: "Yet God has revealed this wisdom to us through the Spirit" (1 Cor. 2:10). As such, it is a door to the understanding of divine reality that could not possibly be known through natural human capabilities. "The natural man does not accept what is taught by the Spirit of God. For him, that is absurdity" (1 Cor. 2:14). In contrast, the "spiritual person," moved and dominated by the Spirit of God, has the key to all of life, not just the earthly dimension. "The spiritual man, on the other hand, can appraise everything, though he himself can be appraised by no one" (1 Cor. 2:15). The source of this Spirit is union with Christ, and identity with him: "For 'Who has known the mind of the Lord so as to instruct him?' But we have the mind of Christ" (1 Cor. 2:16).

The Roots: Baptism and Identity with the Cross

Paul emphasizes in the most vivid possible way the identification of the believer with the death and cross of Christ through baptism.

> Are you not aware that we who were baptized into Christ Jesus were baptized into his death? Through baptism into his death we were buried with him, so that, just as Christ was raised from the dead by the glory of the Father, we too might live a new life [Rom. 6:3–4].

In Chapter 2 we showed the power of the symbolism in the baptismal rite and how it made the believer completely like Christ. Here we wish to emphasize the meaning of association with the death of Christ. Paul explains that it means the death of an old self that was connected to this world and was consequently a slave of sin and the old values of the world. The old self is literally crucified with Christ, because Christ willingly died and separated himself from the world and its power so that he might lead a new completely free risen life in the divine realm. The believer, through faith, willingly unites himself with Christ, "dies," and separates himself from his old life in the world. "This we know: Our old self was crucified with him so that the sinful body might be destroyed and we might be slaves to sin no longer" (Rom. 6:6).

The first effect of this identity with the cross of Christ is a new refreshing sense of freedom. It is a freedom from death, sin, and any earthly power that could possibly stand in the way of or harm a person. "A man who is dead has been freed from sin. If we have died with Christ, we believe that we are also to live with him. We know that Christ, once raised from the dead, will never die again; death has no power over him" (Rom. 6:7–9). In the baptism of a convert from Judaism, the proselyte was considered to begin a new life. Every previous human tie was considered broken. New decisions had to be made in view of the new direction and change in life made possible by the conversion. The same, to a higher degree, was true of Christian baptism. It was so completely an entry into a new life, that it was considered a new creation, a new world, where all the power and bonds of the old world were broken.

The second effect was an intimate association with the cross of Christ in its love for others and life-giving power for all humanity. What Christ did was for all. He made the first break from the limited human condition so that the break might be made possible for all. "The love of Christ impels us who have reached the conviction that since one died for all, all died. He died for all so that those who live might live no longer for themselves, but for him who for their sakes died and was raised up" (2 Cor. 5:14). However, each time a person associates himself or herself with this action, there is a new release of energy, power, and love that goes out to others as an irresistible prayer for them. The duplication of the dying of Christ in one's body also effects an outpouring of life for others as well.

> Continually we carry about in our bodies the dying of Jesus, so that in our bodies the life of Jesus may also be revealed. While we live we are constantly being delivered to death for Jesus' sake, so that the life of Jesus may be revealed in our mortal flesh. Death is at work in us, but life in you [2 Cor. 4:10–12].

The ultimate imitation of the cross is the complete adoption of the role of humble servant of God, which we have previously described. When it is carried out even as far as the cross, and the complete crucifixion of the old self of personal desires, then it becomes completely like that of Christ: "It was thus that he humbled himself, obediently accepting even death, death on the cross" (Phil. 2:8).

Just as Paul saw Jesus carrying his cross precisely for others, he saw himself and the believer willingly bearing the cross, the burdens of others, in order to help them. He writes to the Galatians in reference to those who are weak and have fallen: "Help carry one another's burdens; in that way you will fulfill the Law of Christ" (Gal. 6:2). He saw the cross, the great instrument of pardon and forgiveness for humanity, being extended to more and more people each time a person identified with this essential action: "Be kind to one another, compassionate, and mutually forgiving, just as God has forgiven you in Christ" (Eph. 4:32).

A third effect of identity with the cross was an unshakeable conviction that nothing else was necessary. God's power so completely shown through the nothingness of the cross that the gospel was absolutely sufficient. Nothing else needed to be added, not the slightest detail—even by way of perfection. Paul was so convinced of this that he refused even under heavy pressure to require any further biblical law or observance for Gentile converts. Others might glory in external observances such as circumcision and other religious rites, but he refuses to glory except in the cross of Christ. He will glory only in the wounds and scars in his body that he can show as the results of whippings, floggings, chains, and torture that he has endured in view of the gospel.

> May I never boast of anything but the cross of our Lord Jesus Christ. Through it, the world has been crucified to me and I to the world. It means nothing whether one is circumcised or not. All that matters is that one is created anew. Peace

and mercy on all who follow this rule of life, and
on the Israel of God. Henceforth, let no man
trouble me, for I bear the brand marks of Jesus in
my body [Gal. 6:14–17].

Paul experienced every possible obstacle to the preaching of the gospel: persecution by both Jews and Gentiles,
imprisonment, constant danger to his life, the treachery
of false teachers, physical weakness, etc. (2 Cor.
11:23–28). Among these there was a very serious bodily
impediment that he calls a "thorn of the flesh" (2 Cor.
12:7). We do not know its nature, but it must have been a
constant and humiliating matter, perhaps an embarrassing illness. It bothered him so much that he asked
God again and again to take it away. Yet the request was
denied him in a beautiful answer from God that brought
out that this humiliating obstacle was precisely the best
way that God's power could be shown in the face of
human weakness.

Three times I begged the Lord that this might
leave me. He said to me, "My grace is enough for
you, for in weakness power reaches perfection."
And so I willingly boast of my weaknesses instead that the power of Christ may rest upon me.
Therefore I am content with weakness, with mis-
treatment, with distress, with persecutions and
difficulties for the sake of Christ; for when I am
powerless, it is then that I am strong [2 Cor.
12:10].

The paradox of the cross taught Paul that all the obstacles, events, and people that seemed to upset all his plans
and stand in the way were in fact his best teachers. They
taught him that when all human plans seem to fail, then
it is that the divine plan shines through in a totally unexpected manner. This is why he continually tells his Christians to rejoice in the face of trouble, persecution, and

distress. It is thus that they become most identified with the cross. It is the prelude and instrument for the revelation of God's inner glory already working within themselves and the world: "You in turn became imitators of us and of the Lord, receiving the word despite great trials, with the joy that comes from the Holy Spirit" (1 Thess. 1:6).

To sum up: THE CROSS OF JESUS—everything else in small print!

Reflections for Modern Christians

The cross cuts to the very root of all that is not from God. Hence it is the best remedy for the most insidious sickness of all, which is that of pride in our own efforts and achievements. Even as I write these notes I have the hidden hope that they will be *successful,* that they will win over others somehow. And yet even this is a subtle form of achievement, spiritual though it may be. To hope for success is to hope for something ulterior that results from my own efforts. The cross has nothing ulterior. It allows only that God's power shine through it in surprising ways. Identity with Christ can have no other motivation than *being* identified with him. If I am hung up on tangible results, such as having a group of disciples or influencing others, then I may be deceiving myself. The power of the cross is contagious. It works through me, yet despite my weak efforts.

In reflecting on Paul, there are, however, some signs that point to the sign of the cross:

1. Like Paul, I find myself going out more and more to those who are most needy, afflicted, least likely to give me a return or recompense for what I have done.

2. The sign of the cross is the sign of freedom. Paul had to take great pains to show that this was a freedom from dependence on human discipleship and gurus of all kinds. As you progress in the science of the cross, you will find it to be your best teacher of all. You will become

less dependent on the world, its opinion, and those outside of you. You will have a new criterion for looking at the world and will not fear the judgments of others.

3. Finally, the greatest paradox of all, you will even welcome obstacles, setbacks, opposition, and pain. Most people spend their lives fighting the realities of each day. Endless energy is expended in needless defense. Identity with Christ and the cross changes difficulties into challenges and opportunities. This is because what seems like a setback, a falling apart of our plans, is really the new opening for God's free plan and power to shine despite apparent human failure and weakness. When we are weak, then we are strong, in the expression of Paul. Thus the events or people that make us worry or cause us to be upset are really not stumbling blocks but our best teachers. They teach us to turn within to an entirely new source of power, love, and energy that we can bring into each new situation. This new outflow of dynamic love-energy will work dramatic surprises as the enemy becomes a friend, as the obstacle becomes a great opportunity, as the pain becomes the vehicle for new life. It does not mean that pain and suffering are eliminated. It means that the energy spent fighting them is now no longer lost. Instead it is released, along with added unlimited energy from Christ that will be available to make pain and suffering no longer a liability, but, paradoxically, a great advantage and grace for myself as well as for others.

9

The Secret of
Praying Always

Dialog with God

Paul considered prayer as an absolutely necessary means to accomplish his work. The idea of prayer as an apostolic method coincides with Paul's concept of work. The apostle looked forward to the final completion of God's plan for the world. Since this was God's work, he felt that God alone could accomplish it. Hence he considered prayer as a sine qua non of his apostolic work. Prayer actually brought results. For Paul and all people of faith, it changed the course of events to bring about the fulfillment of God's plan.

All of the Apostle's letters show his absolute confidence in prayer. He never ceases to ask for the prayers of his converts. He asks, first of all, for prayers for specific intentions in connection with the spread of the good news: "that the word of the Lord may make progress and be hailed by many others, even as it has among you. Pray that we may be delivered from confused and evil men" (2 Thess. 3:1), that he might be delivered from great perils (2 Cor. 1:11), that the offering of the Gentile world be acceptable to the Jewish Christians in Jerusalem (Rom. 15:31), and that he might have the opportunity to preach the Word and announce "the mystery of Christ" (Col.

4:3). At other times, he makes general appeals for prayer, e.g., 1 Thess. 5:25: "Brethren, pray for us."

Second, he always assures his converts of his prayers for them, counting on these as really bringing God's action to bear on them. Usually these are prayers for their progress in faith: "that God make you worthy of his calling" (2 Thess. 1:11); "that your love may more and more abound" (Phil. 1:9); other examples: Phil. 1:4; Col. 1:9; 1 Thess. 1:2. He often uses the word, "always" or "unceasingly" to emphasize that he prayed continually for them and to show how important he considered it was for them.

For himself, Paul considered his dialog with God in prayer as the driving force of his life. God was his co-worker, making fruitful his whole work. Hence he felt that intimate communion was essential between himself and the great Person who was shaping his whole life and work. From his letters we can find out how much this meant to his personal life.

The Prayer of Jesus and the Prayer of Paul

The secret of Paul's ability to "pray always" was his deep sense of identity with Christ. The prayer of Jesus himself had been an intimate dialog with God, in which he addressed him as "Abba" (Mark 14:36), the intimate and affectionate word used by children to address their earthly fathers. It was never used to speak to God, where the more solemn Hebrew expression for "father" or "our father" was used. "Abba" was roughly equivalent to "dad," in English. The use of the expression "Abba" by Jesus was so daring and unusual for his time that some people regarded it as blasphemy, an attempt to raise himself to the level of God (John 5:18).

Through the gift of the Spirit, Paul felt he could pray to God in the same daring and confident way that Jesus had. After all, the Spirit made him one with Jesus. Consequently, Paul could write to the Galatians: "God has sent forth into our hearts the spirit of his Son which cries out 'Abba!' ('Father!')'' (Gal. 4:6). It is interesting to note that Paul is using the Aramaic word *Abba* in writing to a Greek audience that does not know Aramaic or Hebrew. This shows that he is most anxious to preserve the word because of its intimate association with Jesus himself. This direct and touching manner of dialog with God meant so much to Paul that he refers to the Father over a hundred times in his letters, usually in connection with Jesus. For him God is the Father of Jesus who taught people to pray to him as "Abba." It was through contact with Paul and praying with him that the first Christians learned to pray in the same manner.

This type of prayer that flowed from identity with Jesus was brought into the concrete circumstances of daily life when Paul united it to the essential elements of the spirit of Jewish prayer in which he had been trained from childhood. For a Jew, the great prayer was that of recognition or praise of God at any time he manifested his presence during the course of the events of each day. This usually took the form of a blessing, followed by a statement of the reason that provoked the praise.

Later Jewish piety established a regular formula for such a blessing, which consisted of the words, "Blessed be thou, O Lord, our God, King of the world, who . . ." (then follows the reason for the blessing). The book of *Berakot* (blessings) in the Talmud contains formulas for scores of occasions that could occur in an ordinary day. The early rabbis were fond of saying that a person who did not pronounce a hundred blessings a day was like a heathen.

An example of such a blessing, perhaps the same used by Jesus himself when he broke bread (Matt. 14:19), would be, "Blessed art thou, O Lord, our God, King of the world, who brings forth bread from the earth." The book of *Berakot* lists blessings for throughout the day beginning from the first moment of rising when the Jew would say, "Blessed art thou, O Lord, King of the world, who raises up the dead." The ideal was that of remembrance and constant recognition of God and his goodness. This is well summed up with the first words of Psalm 33(34): "I will bless the Lord at all times; his praise shall be ever in my mouth."

Of all the blessings, the greatest were those reserved for proclaiming God's goodness in promising the messianic kingdom. Even today, they hold a prominent place in the eighteen blessings pronounced by Jews in their daily prayers. In the fourteenth blessing, the congregation prays that the throne of David be restored: "Blessed are thou, O Lord, who rebuildest Jerusalem." For Paul this great promise was now being fulfilled. The greatest moments of his life were the times when he could take "the cup of blessing" (1 Cor. 10:16) into his hands during the Eucharist and pronounce a preface of praise, blessing God for his great intervention in sending his Son to inaugurate the last times.

Since Paul's Greek-speaking communities were not used to the idea of a Semitic "blessing," the Greek word *eucharistein* (give thanks) took its place. In Paul's letters, we find him frequently bursting out, almost spontaneously, into "blessings" or thanksgivings. This must have been typical of his own private prayer. For example, in 1 Thess. 2:13: "We thank God constantly that in receiving his message from us you took it, not as the word of men, but as it truly is, the Word of God." (For other examples cf. Rom. 1:8; 1 Cor. 1:4; Phil. 1:3; 1 Tim. 1:12.) In view of his identity with Christ through the Spirit, Paul was able to transform this type of prayer by making it an address to God the Father through Jesus. It became a means of sanctifying daily action by seeing a deeper dimension of God's activity in all the ordinary events of each day. As a result, Paul could give this direction to the Colossians: "Whatever you do, whether in speech or in action, do it in the name of the Lord Jesus. Give thanks to God the Father through him (Col. 3:17).

The advantages of such a type of prayer are that it is

geared to reality, to some intervention of God, particularly in regard to God's work in history. Thus Paul developed the habit of spontaneously responding to God who was working through human events to further the kingdom. It was a positive, encouraging type of prayer also, in that it always provided new reasons for hope and confidence as God's hand was recognized as working in human affairs and events.

Just as Jesus often spent long periods, even whole nights, in prayer, so Paul also found time for complete absorption in God that brought him into a mystical state of union with God. He cannot describe what happened to him because human words were not able to convey the deep meaning of these times for him. All he can say is that at one time his prayer was so intense and absorbing that he "was snatched up to Paradise to hear words which cannot be uttered, words which no man may speak" (2 Cor. 12:4). This occasion was only one time out of many, since he refers to "visions and revelations of the Lord" (2 Cor. 12:1).

Guidance by the Holy Spirit and Consultation with God

Flexa quod est rigidum, "bend that which is rigid." These words are from an old Latin hymn to the Holy Spirit, *Veni Sancte Spiritus.* They manifest a quality of the Spirit of Jesus that Paul always sought to capture. The work of God could never be accomplished by any predetermined human means or system; it always remained the initiative of God. This God was a God of history, always acting and intervening in human affairs. He had intervened in Jesus to give people a definite goal of human history. He had also determined to work with and through people to accomplish this goal; they were to be his co-workers.

There were two principal ways by which Paul sought guidance by the Spirit. The first was by prayer, which we have just discussed. The second was through God's action in history and in the events of his life. This second way was built on his conviction that it was most essential for him to study how God at this moment was acting in the world. In what follows we will attempt to point out some situations and problems where Paul was able to discern the will of God and the action of the Spirit by remaining flexible and open to how God manifested himself in concrete situations and crises.

When Paul first began his mission tours, he worked on the principle held by the Jerusalem community. This was that the Jews must first believe in the Messiah, and then would come the conversion of the Gentile world. So Paul then preached the Word first to his countrymen in the synagogue, concentrating his attention on them. There were always a number of Gentile converts, it is true, but they were regarded as the exception to the rule. As Paul journeyed from city to city, it became more and more evident that the Jewish diaspora was not going to respond in great numbers to the preaching of the Word. On the contrary, they offered him the most bitter opposition; far from being a cause of the Gentiles' conversion, they were doing everything possible to hinder it.

Finally in Corinth, the whole matter came to a crisis and Paul decided to change his approach completely. In Corinth (Acts 18) Paul started in his usual way, teaching in the synagogue every Sabbath. He was completely disheartened at the response. The account in Acts reads:

> When they opposed him and insulted him, he would shake his garments in protest and say to them, "Your blood be on your own heads; I am not to blame. From now on, I will turn to the Gentiles." Later Paul withdrew and went into the house of a Gentile named Titus Justus, who reverenced God; his house was next door to the synagogue [Acts 18:6–7].

So instead of making the synagogue or a Jewish home his

center of preaching, he went to a Gentile home, an action that indicated a complete break with his previous approach. Much the same experience was repeated at Ephesus (Acts 19). After three months of very limited success through preaching in the synagogue, Paul withdrew from the synagogue and made his center of preaching the lecture hall of a certain Greek named Tyrannus.

Through experience, then, Paul learned that the Jewish people were not going to respond in great numbers to the preaching of the gospel. It would be the Gentile world that would receive the good news. How did Paul regard this complete reversal of his own expectations and those of the Jerusalem community? He reasoned in this way: The Spirit of Jesus was working in him. If the Jews did not respond, it must be that the Holy Spirit for some purpose did not want them to do so at this time. It was impossible that God's saving purpose should fail. If his work was fruitless in this area, it must be that God willed it for some greater purpose—that somehow, through this rejection, a greater number might be saved.

In the Epistle to the Romans, Chapters 9–11, we find Paul's solution to the problem. God had permitted this temporary blindness of the Jews so that he might concentrate his work on the Gentile world and receive into the church a vast multitude of believers; these would arouse the jealousy of the Jews, who would then enter the church before the Parousia. In other words, God permitted the temporary nonbelief of some, so that he might better have mercy on all. Paul came to this solution because of his openness to the Holy Spirit. He saw that the way God acted through him was an indication of his plans; he was then ready to revise his whole approach in order to conform to God's plans as they revealed themselves in action.

Another important change in Paul's outlook was in regard to the time of the Parousia. Some Jewish traditions seem to have made him believe that the interval between the triumph of the Messiah and the end of the world and resurrection of the dead would be a short period of time. Naturally, then, he looked forward to being alive at the time of the great triumph of Christ. In 1 Thess. 4:15 he includes himself among those alive awaiting the return of Christ: " . . . we who live, who survive until his coming. . . ." Before this, there was to be persecution and suffering, to be sure, but this was the final purification and tribulation, the expected birthpangs heralding the return of the Messiah.

Here again Paul was willing to do some rethinking in view of the working of the Holy Spirit. Some unexpected events prompted him to reconsider many things. More than once he found himself at death's door. At Ephesus, for a time, he was almost sure that he would not escape alive (2 Cor. 1:8–11). The years were passing by without the significant number of Jewish converts that would herald the final days before the Parousia. All this made him take a new look at his view of God's plan. He was certain that God himself had permitted these things to happen and was telling him something through these events. As a result, Paul began to have a new outlook on the suffering and persecution he was undergoing; they were not the final purification before an imminent Parousia, as he had previously thought. He saw them now in a new light; they were the "sufferings of Christ" which Jesus wished to undergo in his members in every place where the gospel was to be preached (Col. 1:24). The time element before the Parousia became less and less important. He began to see his sufferings and even possibly his death in view of his union with Christ in his mission to save people:

> While we live, we are constantly being delivered to death for Jesus' sake, so that the life of Jesus may be revealed in our mortal flesh. Death is at work in us, but life in you" [2 Cor. 4:11–12].

To sum up: For Paul, prayer was truly an apostolic *method,* for it brought certain results through touching the inner divine core moving behind the events of history. He constantly prayed for his converts and begged their intercession as well. His own personal prayer and communion with God as "Abba," Father, was the vital sustaining force in his work. He learned to "pray always" by combining this with traditional Jewish forms of prayer. Paul looked for the inner guidance of the Spirit both through prayer and alertness to the work of the Spirit in the important moments of everyday life.

Applications for Modern Christians

When we consider Paul, it seems so obvious that modern apostles must be a people of prayer. The whole work of the apostolate today is just as much a pure work of faith as it was in the first century. And the only dialog that can sustain and nourish that faith is prayer. However, we might add that it was easier to pray in ancient times than today. In those days, the divine world seemed always so close and ready to burst out into the visible world. Not knowing the laws of science, people in the first century saw the universe as a great mystery where God was always working as a first cause in his work of providence.

Today many people no longer look at the world in the same way. The well-ordered laws of science seem to remove much of the air of mystery and awe that surrounded the world in the eyes of first century men and women. This means that we must make a greater effort to recover the deep sense of mystery in human beings and the universe. This will mean devoting "prime time" each day to meditation and prayer to counteract the strong, materialistic view of the world we find around us.

As for Paul, frequent periods of long prayer are necessary today both to refresh the apostle and provide the only source of strength adequate for an authentic Christian lifestyle. Since our outlook on the world and events tends so much to be "secular," that is, excluding God's hand, we must remind ourselves continually that the God we believe in is a God of history, who does not act in the abstract but in the "ordinary" events of each day. In view of this tendency to secularization, Paul's prayer of "blessing" or recognition takes on special importance. It is a prayer that is geared to reality and based on the faith that God is acting in both nature and history. This type of prayer can be frequent, intense, as well as very natural. For apostles who pray in this manner, no day can be an "ordinary" day, for they will always be alert and ready every day for new interventions on the part of God.

I will always remember a young apostle who asked a very successful missionary to share with him some of the techniques that were responsible for his numerous converts and the rapid growth of his Christian community. Quite simply the missionary replied that the first and most important thing he did before approaching a new group of people was to start an intense campaign of prayer, not only in his immediate community but even to the extent of writing to request the prayers of friends and other Christian communities. The young man had not expected that answer. He countered somewhat impatiently, "All right, now tell me what you really do." The missioner replied, "But that is what I *really* do." This man understood well that unless a person believes that prayer really matters, it is not really prayer at all.

10

Herald of the Word

Paul's View of Preaching

There is a striking difference between Paul's idea of preaching and the common popular meaning of the word. For the ordinary person, the word "preaching" is generally associated with the "homily" in a liturgical assembly where usually only believers are present. Paul's own view is much more personal, dynamic, and meaningful.

In Paul's time, when the emperor or some public authority wished to announce to the people an important message affecting their lives he employed a herald or town crier who would arrive in town, blow a trumpet, and announce in a loud voice an authoritative message from the ruling powers. It was really not the messenger who spoke; he was only an instrument for the voice of the ruler to reach the people. He did not speak of his own convictions, but was a mouthpiece or agent of the king. He had to announce an important truth that would affect the lives of all his hearers.

With this in mind, we can see how Paul understood himself as a preacher. As a preacher, he was chosen herald to announce an urgent message from God himself that would affect the destiny of all humankind. It simply *had* to be made known to everyone. God had entrusted

Paul to announce a message of reconciliation to the whole world:

> God, in Christ, was reconciling the world to himself, not counting men's transgressions against them, and . . . he has entrusted the message of reconciliation to us [2 Cor. 5:19].

The message he spoke was authoritative, from God himself, not a matter of personal conviction or opinion:

> That is why we thank God constantly that in receiving his message from us you took it, not as the word of men but as it truly is, the Word of God . . . [1 Thess. 2:13].

The message confided to him was so important that people's response to it would determine their whole future:

> We are an aroma of Christ for God's sake both among those who are saved and those on the way to destruction; to the latter, an odor dealing death, but to the former, a breath bringing life [2 Cor. 2:15–16].

The object and content of the message was not a piece of information but a world-shaking event: God had begun his final intervention in history through the death and resurrection of Jesus. This is so essential that the whole meaning of preaching vanishes if this event is not certain: "If Christ has not been raised, our preaching is void of content and your faith is empty, too" (1 Cor. 15:14).

The message has nothing abstract in it; people are intimately involved. If people are united to Christ in faith, his victory becomes theirs:

Our faith will be credited to us also if we believe
in him who raised Jesus our Lord from the dead,
the Jesus who was handed over for our sins, and
raised up for our justification [Rom. 4:25].

Once the great event is announced, how can people
enter into it? Paul does not see preaching as simply
"talking at" people, but as a real dialog to which people
give a human response. Preaching is a confrontation
between the divine "I" and the human "thou." The
preacher is the instrument through which God speaks to
people in a real communication of friendship with those
who are open to this message and give it their human
assent and cooperation. It is through confrontation with
God in a dialog of friendship that people enter into the
earthshaking event that changes both their own lives and
the course of the world.

Paul considers preaching as being absolutely essential
to the dialog of faith: "It pleased God to save those who
believe by the absurdity of the preaching of the Gospel"
(1 Cor. 1:21). In Romans, Paul affirms that people cannot
be saved unless preachers, authoritative messengers, be
sent in order to announce to people the good news:

How can they believe unless they have heard of
him? And how can they hear, unless there is
someone to preach? And how can men preach
unless they are sent? . . . Faith, then, comes
through hearing, and what is heard is the Word
of Christ [Rom. 10:14–17].

We may conclude then that Paul saw no way for men
and women to enter into God's saving event in Christ
except through preaching an example. God had intervened in human history and had decided that this great
event be made known to people through commissioned
human messengers through whom he would speak.

Those who responded to the proclamation in real dialog could enter into relation with the God who spoke and thus become involved in his great plan for the world.

Characteristics of Paul's Preaching

If there is one word that could characterize Paul's preaching, it would be the Greek word *parresia*, which means a certain boldness, assurance, and confidence. In 2 Cor. 4:13 he writes, "Because I believed, I spoke out [Ps. 115:10]. We also believe; therefore we speak out." Since Jesus had given him his own Spirit, the Spirit of God, Paul was sure that he must "speak out" and bring the good news of God's great saving event to others.

Paul understood the active meaning of "Spirit" from his study of the Bible. Here he saw that "Spirit" meant God himself who worked in creation, especially in human beings. He saw that the gift of the Spirit was not static—something a person just "rested" in. It was always dynamic; it moved people either to speak with assurance about things beyond human knowledge, or to act suddenly with a strength beyond that of human beings. He had read of times when the Spirit of God came upon people, especially the prophets, and they spoke of the wondrous deeds of God. He thought of how the Spirit suddenly seized King Saul, who amazed everyone by starting to prophesy ecstatically (1 Sam. 10:10). He remembered how the Spirit of the Lord came upon David when he was anointed king, enabling him to be a mighty ruler (1 Sam. 16:13).

As a student of the Law, Paul knew that God had promised literally to pour out his Spirit on people in the messianic times. For Joel the Prophet had written,

> Afterward, I will pour out my spirit upon all mankind. Your sons and daughters shall prophesy, your old men shall dream dreams, your young men shall see visions [Joel 3:1].

When Saul the Pharisee saw the risen, exalted Jesus on the road to Damascus, he knew that this time had come. The risen Messiah, at the right hand of God, had poured this Spirit into the church that he had been persecuting. Ananias, the head of the Christian community at Damascus, told Paul,

> Saul, my brother, I have been sent by the Lord Jesus who appeared to you on the way here, . . . that you may be filled with the Holy Spirit [Acts 9:17].

So this is why Jesus appeared to him—to give him the fullness of the Spirit that was promised for the final messianic times.

The gift of the Spirit moved him to "speak out." "Straightway in the synagogues of Damascus he began to preach that Jesus was the Son of God" (Acts 9:20). In fact he was so outspoken and declared his case so forcibly that "the Jews made a plot to kill him" (Acts 9:23). Since the Jews were guarding the gates night and day to kill him, his disciples succeeded in saving him only by putting him in a basket and lowering him secretly over the wall. The incident was always an embarrassing one to Paul, the fact that he, a short man, had to literally be stuffed into a basket in order to save his skin! Writing to the Corinthians, he retells the story with considerable emotion (2 Cor. 11:31–33).

On reaching Jerusalem he tried to join the company of the disciples, but even they were afraid of him; they could hardly believe that such a sudden change had come about in their worst enemy. Barnabas, however, took him into the community meeting and told them how Paul had seen the Lord and how he had *expressed himself openly* in the name of Jesus. Whenever Luke uses this Greek verb *parresiazomai* or the noun from the same root, *parresia,* it is usually in connection with preaching. By it he means a fearlessness, openness, and assurance that accompanies the preaching of the certain message that the risen Jesus had sent his Spirit into the church and was mightily at work preparing for his final return in triumph.

Throughout the Acts of the Apostles, Luke refers to this characteristic *parresia* of Paul. In Jerusalem, Paul had taken such a confident and bold stand that Jesus was the long-awaited Messiah that his listeners were quick to react. Jerusalem became too "hot" for Paul. The brethren were fearful both for Paul and for themselves and sent him home.

Here at Jerusalem we observe a certain pattern that Paul's entry into a new region will take: His presentation of the Good News will be so forceful that his audience will quickly take a stand, one way or the other. Luke notes the same characteristic of Paul's preaching at Antioch (Acts 13:46) and at Iconium (Acts 14:3). Here he notes that the boldness of Paul's preaching is due to the Spirit of the risen Jesus; it is a boldness "of the Lord." Paul and Barnabas spent considerable time there and spoke out fearlessly in complete reliance on the Lord. The Lord for his part confirmed the message with his grace and caused signs and wonders to be done at their hands. The same description is used of Paul's preaching at Ephesus (Acts 19:8).

Luke sees the career of the Apostle reach a triumphant peak at Rome. In the last verse of Acts Luke writes, "with full assurance, and without any hinderance whatever, he preached the reign of God, welcomed all who came to him preaching the kingdom of God and taught about the Lord Jesus Christ" (Acts 28:31). Thus the evangelist begins and ends his description of the preaching career of Paul with an emphasis on this characteristic *parresia*.

What was the source of this unusual assurance and enthusiasm with which Paul spoke? The source was none less than Jesus himself. During his earthly life, Jesus himself had spoken with that same assurance and certainty when he spoke of his passion, death, and return to establish his kingdom.

> He began to teach them that the Son of Man had to suffer much, . . . be put to death, and rise three days later. He said these things quite openly [with *parresia,* in the Greek; Mark 8:31–32].

Now that he had risen from the dead, the Son of Man was pouring his own Spirit into the messianic community, a Spirit that brought this same openness and assurance *(parresia).*

Even the enemies of the early church recognized that Peter and John had captured this characteristic quality of Jesus.

> Observing the self-assurance [*parresia*] of Peter and John and realizing that the speakers were uneducated men of no standing, the questioners were amazed. They recognized these men as having been with Jesus [Acts 4:13].

The early community at Jerusalem recognized this boldness or assurance as the special work of the Spirit of Jesus, for they make special mention of it in their prayers:

> Now, O Lord, look at the threats they are leveling against us. Grant to your servants, even as they speak your words, complete assurance . . . [Acts 4:29].

Their prayers were promptly answered, for

> the place where they were gathered shook as they prayed. They were all filled with the Holy Spirit and continued to speak God's word with *confidence* [Acts 4:31].

Paul himself attributed this *parresia* or confidence to the risen Jesus, who on the way to Damascus had called him, chosen him, and literally seized him. Now he was the instrument and mouthpiece of the risen Lord, who had chosen to bring about his final triumph in people through human instruments. Hence the divine power was truly at work in his words, which had the power of those of God himself.

It would be well for us to outline some of the features and content of this *parresia* which was so characteristic of Paul:

1. An essential part of this *parresia* was a certain hope of resurrection that was based on the possession of the identical Spirit that raised up and was raising Jesus himself from the dead. Paul was always preaching about the Resurrection as the central point of his whole life of faith. So much so that he writes,

> If there is no resurrection of the dead, Christ himself has not been raised. And if Christ has not been raised, our preaching is void of content and your faith is empty too [1 Cor. 15:13]. . . . If our hopes in Christ are limited to this life only, we are the most pitiable of men [1 Cor. 15:19].

For him the amazing truth was that he could have the same hope of rising from the dead that Jesus himself had, since he possessed the same Spirit that was in Jesus. He expresses this to the Romans not as an opinion or a possibility but as the firmest of all assurances:

> If the Spirit of him who raised Jesus from the dead dwells in you, then he who raised Jesus Christ from the dead will bring your mortal bodies to life also through his Spirit dwelling in you [Rom. 8:11].

This hope was not for a solitary resurrection in Christ. It was always concerned with a community resurrection in him. Even when many miles of journey separated Paul from his Christians, he was always conscious that they shared the same Spirit and that this Spirit would bring about a joyful reunion with one another at the Resurrection. It was this hope that animated him in his worst trials. During a very severe persecution at Ephesus, when he feared he might not see his friends at Corinth again, he wrote to them, "He who raised up the Lord Jesus will raise us up also along with Jesus and will place both us and you in his presence" (2 Cor. 4:14).

Because the Spirit of the risen Jesus was actually in possession of the Christian and not merely something to be hoped for, Paul likes to call the Spirit an actual pledge of the Resurrection. Writing to the Corinthians, he yearns to be clothed over with a new resurrection body and exclaims, "God has fashioned us for this very thing and has given us the Spirit as a pledge of it" (2 Cor. 5:5).

2. At the root of Paul's bold assurance and confidence was the extraordinary gift of being able to address God in the same unique way that Jesus did—as *Father.* As noted above in Chapter 9, the greatest secret of Jesus was the power he had to address God himself as *Abba* (Mark 14:36). This Aramaic word was the familiar term that Jewish children of his time used to address their earthly fathers. In liturgical prayer, the more formal Hebrew word for "father" was more commonly used. The enemies of Jesus were quick to take notice that there was something very unusual about his frequent and very intimate references to his Father (John 5:18).

For Paul, the greatest privilege of his life was the ability that the risen Jesus had given him to likewise say, "Abba, father." For him it was so simple: God had sent his Son so that he and his *brothers and sisters* might become children as well:

> When the designated time came, God sent forth
> his Son, born of a woman . . . that we might
> receive our status as adopted sons. The proof
> that you are sons is the fact that God has sent

forth into our hearts the Spirit of his Son which
cries out, "Abba, Father" [Gal. 4:4–7].

Although he was now addressing a Greek audience
that did not know Aramaic, Paul was anxious to preserve
the exact word that Jesus himself had used to show that
this was now the unique privilege of a Christian. The
expression "our father" or "the father" became Paul's
most favorite expression in prayer; he uses it some fifty
times in his epistles, identifying frequently "our father"
with the "father of our Lord Jesus Christ, to show that
this is a gift that comes through Christ" (e.g., 1 Thess.
1:1; Col. 1:1–3).

Paul understood that this unique privilege must now
be shared with many new brothers and sisters. He felt
that he had something to give, a Spirit that could be
shared. This could be a tremendous motivation both for
himself and for others who would be drawn to the
church. His "method" was something he had—a Spirit
to be shared. Consequently, he described his conversion
in these words, "It pleased him . . . to reveal his Son in
me, that I might preach him among the Gentile world"
(Gal. 1:16). God had given him the Spirit of his Son, so
what could he do but announce this to the whole world
and give them the same opportunity!

3. This gift of the Spirit of God's Son likewise had the
effect of opening up a vast future to all men and women.
What God had in store for the world was now revealed to
Paul: He wished to bring every person in the world to
true communion by this Spirit. The Spirit had only begun
to work in people during this earthly life; it would continue to work and bring out a glorious transformation at
the Resurrection. Then Paul and others would completely share the sonship of Jesus in a risen body. Jesus
himself was only the "firstborn among many brothers"
(Rom. 8:29) through his Resurrection. Many were to follow him. This is the eager longing of all creation, "the
final revelation of the sons of God" (Rom. 8:19).

This unfolding of God's eternal plan was a great point in Paul's witness and preaching, for it brought a certain knowledge of what the future held for those who believed. In his later years, the Apostle would refer to this as a mystery that God was now revealing through his preaching:

> . . . to preach among you his word in its fullness—that mystery hidden from ages and generations, but now revealed to his holy ones. God has willed to make known to them the glory beyond price which this mystery brings to the Gentiles, the mystery of *Christ in you,* your hope of glory [Col. 1:26–27].

To sum up: For Paul, preaching itself was an essential activity of an apostle. It was the means that God had chosen to enable people both to discover and to share in his plan for a new world. Paul's preaching was characterized by *parresia,* a boldness and assurance that came from his absolute confidence that God was speaking and working through him. Basic to this *parresia* was his assurance of a community resurrection in Jesus as well as his certainty of a new relation of sonship with God and kinship with all people. This gave the key to God's plan for the future.

Applications for Modern Apostles

"I have been made its herald and apostle" (1 Tim. 2:7). As a herald, Paul contributed to the rapid expansion of the church by continually proclaiming the good news to new groups of people in new places. Today, most preaching occurs in liturgical celebrations as a homily *to believers* after the reading of the gospel. If the Church is not expanding today at the rate it should, this points to an urgent necessity of obtaining more preachers of the good news to *nonbelievers* in new areas.

We say *nonbelievers* because the very mission of Christ on earth was to attract and help them. Christ was "the faithful witness" (Apoc. 1:5). A witness is one who exists primarily for another. The church, those who do believe, must likewise witness: "You are to be my witnesses" (Acts 1:8). As such, sharing the mission of Christ, the church exists not only for itself but for others, those who do not yet believe. In fact the best way to grow in the Spirit is to be continually helping others to grow also. In this way we renew and deepen our own experience of the Spirit. The best way, likewise, to grow stale is to keep it to ourselves as if it were a private possession. What we have been given is a precious privilege to be shared by all.

We say *new areas* because in almost any locality there is some good ground, already prepared, that will produce an abundant harvest for the seed of the Word. The other ground may take some time to prepare; meanwhile the local harvesters will provide seed for it when the time comes. It would be a mistake to leave other good ground in other areas waiting long periods of time, and thus cut off hopes of rapid growth of the church.

The characteristic *parresia* of Paul had a profound influence on the people he contracted. To people overwhelmed with fear and uncertainty, Paul held out the opportunity of a real strength, certainty, and assurance that came from a Person he could share with others. Today the world is faced with the same uncertainties. Technical progress has not enabled people to face the basic problems of suffering and death, nor given them the strength they need to work selflessly for a better world. Modern apostles must strip themselves of everything that would hinder the powerful witness of a faith that points to absolute assurance and confidence in God alone. This will mean a real poverty of spirit that will be reflected in a true poverty of life. Real *parresia* or assurance in God can be perfectly realized only when all worldly assurance is put aside. Apostles must be members of the church of the poor that is rich only in God.

Only then will the world stop doubting their motives and see clearly their witness.

This *parresia*, or boldness, from the Spirit proceeds from a deep conviction of the truth, and the desire to take a stand on this publicly and openly. This truth is not just a matter of spiritual or religious experience. It concerns God's own justice which is part of his nature. It will mean taking a courageous and open stand on behavior and practices whether by government, groups, or individuals that go contrary to God's intention to bring justice, oneness, fairness, and equality on earth. This stand must be public not private, because injustice is not private but public. This concern for the truth will take practical measures to see that the truth is heard and manifest to as many people as possible. It will mean publicity through letters, speeches, advertisements, literature, or whatever means that are apt to the end. Paul was even willing to go to prison with the assurance that what he believed in would reach an even wider audience!

11

The Radiating Center of the Apostolate

While individual contacts and personal friendships marked the beginnings of a new church, it was through the Greek "household" that the new faith spread rapidly in Paul's world. The Greek *oikos* or *oikia* formed the basic social unit that was best fitted for the extension of the church. There is no exact equivalent in Greek for the English word "family." The *oikos*, or household, was a kind of extended family, many of whom lived together. It was composed not only of members of the family (in our sense) but also of employees, slaves, tenants, and other dependents.

The master or mistress of the household ruled over all, and his or her decisions even in religious matters had a great effect on all, since religious worship was essential to every household. The New Testament has many examples of the influence exercised by the head of the household. The Roman Cornelius was "religious and God-fearing." The same was true of his whole household (Acts 10:2). At Philippi, Paul's jailor took him and Silas to his home; "they proceeded to announce the Word of God to him and to everyone in his house" (Acts 16:32). Luke records that the jailor was baptized and "his whole household" (Acts 16:33). John's Gospel notes the influence that the royal official at Capernaum exerted on his household: "He and his whole household thereupon became believers" (John 4:53).

From the Acts of the Apostles and the Epistles we see that Paul's approach was often through some influential member of a community, whose household would then become a church center. At Philippi, there was a Greek woman named Lydia, of some means, who "already reverenced God" (Acts 16:14), i.e., was perhaps already attached to Jewish worship. When she had listened to Paul, she asked to be baptized, and Luke records that her household was baptized also (Acts 16:15). Her house then became a center of the church at Philippi. Paul and Silas consented to live there and when they were released from prison they returned to her house where they saw the brethren and encouraged them (Acts 16:14). At Thessalonica, it was Jason and his house who received the apostles, and also bore the brunt of the persecution (Acts 17:5–9).

At Corinth, the president of the synagogue, Crispus, was baptized together with his household (Acts 18:8). His house provided ready access to those Jews who joined the church. Paul however moved to the house of Titus Justus, a Gentile "who reverenced God," who lived next door. Titus had been attracted by the synagogue, but of course could not obtain full membership without circumcision. His position made it easier for Gentile converts to come to his house. Paul also notes that he baptized the household of Stephanas (1 Cor. 1:16). He calls the latter's household and that of Fortunatus, "the first fruits of Achaia" (1 Cor. 16:15). The house of Gaius was also very prominent. In Rom 16:23 Paul refers to him as his own host and that of the whole church.

At Ephesus the household of Priscilla and Aquila became a center of the church. Writing to Corinth from their home, Paul says, "Aquila and Priscilla together with the assembly that meets in their house send you cordial greetings in the Lord. All the brothers greet you" (1 Cor.

16:19; cf. Rom. 16:3). At Colossae, the house of Philemon became a church (Philem. 2), while at Laodicae, the house of Nymphas earned the same distinction (Col. 4:15).

While we cannot give a detailed outline of how Paul worked through the "household of the faith" (Gal. 6:10) we can point to some consequences of this family-centered approach:

1. The family nature of the new faith was easily inculcated within this compact social unit. New Christians quickly recognized the deep fraternal union that had its source in the Eucharist celebrated in the home. The Passover service had been essentially a family celebration; now the Eucharist took its place, and converts saw the Lord's Supper as truly a family meal with the risen Jesus. Temples and buildings were not needed since the home had become a temple of living stones built on Christ. There was also a beautiful "smallness" about the Greek household church. Everyone knew one another and reinforced one another as a closely knitted "body of Christ."

2. The Christian "household" helped to promote local responsibility for the church. The offices and duties already exercised in the extended household prepared the way for the responsibilities of the faith. Jesus himself had compared the responsibilities of church leaders to those exercised in a household (Matt. 24:42–51; Mark 13:44–37). Paul noted the new responsibilities taken on a Christian household in Corinth and asked all to cooperate: "It is devoted to the service of the saints. I urge you to serve under such men and under everyone who cooperates and toils with them" (1 Cor. 16:15–16). Also it was possible for Paul to select men and women already recognized for their natural qualities of leadership and give them new responsibilities and opportunities in the church. Responding to this trust, the church at Philippi even took upon themselves the financial support of Paul in his founding of new churches (2 Cor. 11:9; Phil. 1:5; 4:10–15).

3. The Christian *oikos* provided the opportunity for the

gradual breaking down of all social barriers. The unity and equality of all in their new faith, particularly in the celebration of the Last Supper, had far-reaching effects, especially in attracting converts. Master and slave, man and woman, Gentile and Jew were together at the same Eucharistic table. "There does not exist among you Jew or Greek, slave or freeman, male or female. All are one in Christ Jesus" (Gal. 3:28). This new equality in Christ would only slowly penetrate and overcome centuries-old institutions and barriers but the principle of change had begun to infiltrate. Onesimus, the converted slave, becomes Paul's "most dear and faithful brother"; Onesimus's former master is asked to receive him back, "no longer a slave but as more than a slave, a beloved brother" (Philem. 16).

4. In the presentation of doctrine the idea of the "household" was a convenient and easy parallel to explain the nature of the church. Paul describes the latter as "the household of the faith" (Gal. 6:10). Christians are "members of the household of God" (Eph. 2:19). The guidance of a bishop or presbyter over the church is compared to that of a father over his household: "If a man does not know how to manage his own house, how can he take care of the church of God" (1 Tim. 3:6). The church is indeed "God's household" (1 Tim. 3:15).

The parallels extend to the inner nature of the church itself. Jesus is the "first born of many brothers" (Rom. 8:29), to whose image many others must be conformed. Christians are not slaves in God's house, but true heirs of the father. God has adopted them as his own sons, and given all the privileges of sonship:

> You did not receive a spirit of slavery leading you back into fear, but a spirit of adoption through which we cry out, "Abba, Father!" [Rom. 8:15].

The way that Paul and others approached the Greek world appears to be reflected in the Gospels themselves.

The gospel authors had seen how Christian traveling apostles went from place to place, first establishing a center in a home and then radiating outward. The directions of Jesus to his apostles reflect this first-century experience. The Lord tells both the seventy-two and the Twelve not to go from house to house but rather to find a house that will receive them, and then work out from there (Luke 9:4; 10:6–8).

To sum up: Paul made the best possible use of the Greek household as a natural center for the Christian community. This "extended family" helped foster the family covenant bonds of the new faith. It provided an ideal setting for the development of Christian leadership. It also helped to begin the long struggle to break down the deep social barriers that divided the pagan and Jewish world. To outsiders it was a striking and meaningful model of what God wanted in the world. To insiders it was a new home in the deepest possible sense of the word.

Applications for Modern Apostles

For Paul the Greek *oikos* afforded the best way to establish the church in Greek culture. The apostle of today must have the training, skill, and patience necessary to seek in new cultures the most influential vehicle for beginning and developing the church. At this point I am reminded of a time when, as a missionary, I was rather pessimistic about the prospects of winning over a certain country village in the mountains of Guatemala. My catechist simply said to me, "Father, all we need is one house; that's how we started in all these other villages." His observations proved to be correct for the Indian "house" was a rather widely extended family.

In the rapidly developing nations of today, this center of personal influence may be quite varied and at times hard to find. It may be neighborhood block leaders or a political, educational, or business association that exerts a predominating influence. It is important to find people who already command the respect of a certain group because of their reputation for responsibility. Such persons will be prepared to exercise new responsibilities in the community of God and will draw many with them.

While mass media will always remain important, the ultimate goal is the establishment of a true covenant community. However, every covenant community begins with one person or several who take the initiative and feel a real responsibility for others. The apostle must be careful first to seek out those persons best able to understand the family nature and responsibilities of the church.

Putting together Chapter 5 on the nature of the apostle and this chapter on the household church, we can get a blueprint vision of the church of the future. It will be a church deeply convinced that it is the people of God, that each member shares the priesthood of Christ as members of his body. It will be a community where all members have a decision-making role and full opportunity to use their gifts to serve the world.

There will be a large number of small, closely-knit communities where everyone knows one another and contributes to each other's growth. Each will have their own leader, or they may wish to alternate leaders within the community. In view of the family nature of the church, leaders will usually have been married according to the prescription of 1 Tim. 3:2, so that they will have had full opportunity for maturity in responsible family and community life. The task of the community Christian leaders will be principally in the Word of God and as leaders in prayer. They will dedicate themselves to strengthen and encourage brothers and sisters to be all they should be as Christians for the world. Since communities will be small, leaders will be able to support themselves, working in the world, as Paul himself recommended by word and by example (Acts 20:34–35). Since the community will be small enough to meet in private homes, there will not be heavy financial and institutional responsibilities to weigh down the community and keep it from spiritual priorities.

As detailed in Chapter 5, there will be a body of full-time apostles or ministers of the Word. Some will be married; others will be celibates working together as teams. Their main task will be to establish new communities, to coordinate them, and serve their leaders. They will also try to reach and influence areas where the local church cannot extend itself. They will have no financial burdens and responsibilities. Their ministry will be entirely spiritual, since the "small church" has no need of buildings and institutions to support it. The support of the body of full-time apostles will be the joint responsibility of all of the many small communities.

In my own personal experience, my wife and I have found it helpful to set aside one definite evening each week when we invite people to join us for a reading (usually from Scriptures), a period of silent reflection, a time of prayer for one another's concerns, and a symbolic sharing of bread and wine. Those who wish to continue thus find a definite place, time, and community where they can experience the power of the Spirit. For us, this has been the beginning of many friendships and associations that have endured over the years and have been an instrument for the development of Christian communities. The home, as Paul found out, is the best place to start.

12

The Diamond of Diversity

"All things to all men" (1 Cor. 9:22).

One of Paul's greatest gifts was the ability to see the one Spirit of God working in the whole human race like a bright light shining through a sparkling diamond. Each of the many sides transmits, diffuses, and filters this light according to the special qualities and angles of the jewel. Thus Paul was able to love and appreciate people of many diverse backgrounds despite the differences of race and religion that alienated them from others. Paul loved the Gentiles as lost and separated brothers and sisters. He especially cherished his own Jewish people despite heart-rending conflicts at times. He was able to be on good terms with Christians in his own communities whose orientation and lifestyle was quite different from his own.

The Apostle of the Gentiles: His Love for the Non-Jewish and Non-Christian World

There is no title that is so unique to Paul as that of apostle or teacher of the Gentile world. There is no doubt that he felt especially drawn to the Gentiles. On the other side, the Gentiles were able to detect this inner attraction and come to him as a teacher despite all the cultural shock they experienced in associating with and following a person whose whole life and training had been in Jewish custom and law. The roots of Paul's attraction to the Gentiles were deep in his heart. As a student of Scripture, he had come to understand God's love for the whole human race as his one family. If there was one God, there simply had to be one family of humankind. Paul felt that his special work was to bring together once more the separated, alienated, and scattered people in the world so that together they could call on the one God in prayer while recognizing their inner kinship. For Paul, Christ was the great agent of oneness who would cause people to discover their inner oneness-space and deepen it to new dimensions made possible by the Spirit of God. The final state would be as expressed in Romans 10: 12–13:

> Here there is no difference between Jew and Greek; all have the same Lord, rich in mercy toward all who call upon him. "Everyone who calls on the name of the Lord will be saved."

Notice the universal, yet unified tone of this message: no differences, all with the same Lord, who is filled with mercy toward *all*—a God who wants *everyone* to be free to call upon him.

Paul's appreciation of this deep inner oneness of all people goes back to his understanding of creation. He sees that every person has a hidden inner divine element that makes oneness a reality. This is life itself. Life is so much a gift from God and a sharing of divine life that the author of Genesis describes God as taking clay into his hands, modeling it into the form of a person and then blowing his own breath into it in order to give it life (Gen. 2:7). Paul quotes this verse as he thinks back on Adam the first person as a model of human nature. Paul sees this basic oneness as a preparation for a greater oneness that is to result through Christ: "Adam, the first man, became a living soul; the last Adam has become a life-giving spirit" (1 Cor. 15:45).

In addition to this, Paul looked upon the whole universe as a shining manifestation of God to every human being on earth. God was not a far off being, but someone whose presence permeated the whole world and could be evident in all creation, especially people. In fact, whatever can be known about God is clear to them; he himself made it so. "Since the creation of the world, invisible realities, God's eternal power and divinity, have become visible, recognized through the things he has made" (Rom. 1:20).

Paul did not see a discontinuity between God as the creating light of the universe and the light of the Spirit that illuminated Christ and his disciples. One led to the other. It was the same God who created light from darkness who shone on the face of Christ and through him to others: "For God, who said, 'Let light shine out of darkness,' has shone in our hearts, that we in turn might make known the glory of God shining on the face of Christ" (2 Cor. 4:6).

From Paul's letters, we do not know how Paul spoke to non-Jewish audiences. However, Luke in the Acts of the Apostles (17:22–32) provides us with what he considers to be Paul's typical approach to such an audience. This was the occasion when Paul was forced to remain alone at Athens and was invited to give a lecture in the Areopagus. The central theme of the lecture is God's living presence in the world, especially through human beings in whom he has placed an essential oneness. However, all human history has an inner direction leading to the present time where God has sent one man, Jesus, whom he has raised from the dead in order to judge the present world and begin a new unified humanity.

Paul begins his talk with reference to an altar he had discovered that was dedicated "To a God Unknown."

For him, this is the hidden one God whom he worships. His presence is evident to all the world; he is not confined to human temples or sanctuaries: "For the God who made the world and all that is in it, the Lord of heaven and earth, does not dwell in sanctuaries made by human hands" (Acts 17:24). This God is intimately connected to all human beings as the divine source of life-breath to all creatures: "It is he who gives to all life and breath and everything else" (Acts 17:25). In addition he has placed an essential oneness within people: "From one stock he made every nation of mankind to dwell on the face of the earth" (Acts 17:26). Because of these divine elements in people, there is a natural movement and seeking of the God who is not far off, but so near to each one: "They were to seek God, yet to grope for him and perhaps eventually to find him—though he is not really far from any one of us. 'In him we live and move and have our being,' as some of your own poets have put it, 'for we too are his offspring' " (Acts 17:28). Yet in addition to God as the creating and sustaining presence in the universe, he is also a God of history moving the world from within according to a certain plan: "Now he calls on all men everywhere to reform their lives. He has set the day on which he is going to 'judge the world with justice' through a man he has appointed—one whom he has endorsed in the sight of all by raising him from the dead" (Acts 17:30–31). In other words, a new age is dawning in which all people must face judgment and be ready to come together once more in justice and peace.

For Paul, then, the Gentiles were not aliens and strangers. They were lost brothers and sisters. God's own love was the impelling force to search for them and bring them back to God's family. The Apostle saw a deep inner mystery of God's plan, power, and love working in the Gentile world to bring every person back to the oneness-space God has already created in their hearts. In writing to Gentiles, he calls this mystery "Christ in you, your hope of glory" (Col. 1:27).

Paul and Israel: "Has God Rejected His People?
Of Course Not!" (Rom. 11:1)

Throughout his life, Paul had deep affection in his heart for his fellow Jews even though he felt pain and grief in his heart that they had not joined him in believing in Christ.

> I speak the truth in Christ: I do not lie. My con-
> science bears me witness in the Holy Spirit that
> there is great grief and constant pain in my heart.
> Indeed, I could even wish to be separated from
> Christ for the sake of my brothers, my kinsmen
> the Israelites [Rom. 9:1–3].

Although they have not joined him in Christ, Paul still regards God's presence and work in Israel as something permanent and enduring: "Has God rejected *his* people? Of course not!" (Rom. 11:1). He takes care to point out that they have the covenant, the glory of the presence of God, meaningful worship, as well as being the very stock and race of the Messiah.

> Theirs were [are, in Greek] the adoption, the
> glory, the covenant, the law-giving, the wor-
> ship, and the promises; theirs were the patri-
> archs, and from them came the Messiah. (I speak
> of his human origins.) Blessed forever be God
> who is over all! [Rom. 9:4–5].

For Paul, the Jews are not a dried-up root of Christianity. On the contrary, the Jews are the rich live root of the olive tree to which Gentile Christians have been grafted on as branches. If the root dies, the branches also die. Such is the vitality and importance of the Jewish people that Christians cannot do without them. In fact, Paul believes that when the Jewish people in large numbers do join them, it will be such a tremendous influx of new life and vitality that it will be similar to a resurrection from the dead (Rom. 11:15).

Wherever Paul went, he always went first to the Jewish synagogue, where he stayed and was welcomed as a Jewish rabbi and teacher from Jerusalem. The bitter opposition of the majority of Jews to Paul was not due to his belief in Jesus as Messiah, but due to the fact that he welcomed Gentiles as full members of the messianic community without any of the biblical and traditional laws that distinguished Jewish belief. This was simply too much for most to bear—after all, the promise was made to the Jewish people. The Messiah was a Jewish Messiah. They could not feel at home in a community where there were Gentiles who did not respect and keep the Torah, especially the many laws about food and purity. Naturally, Paul deeply felt this animosity and fully experienced the pain of separation from his fellow Jews. But the reason for the pain was not a feeling that Jews were rejected or excluded by God, but because Paul knew they were impeding his work among the Gentiles by their opposition. Indeed, the great project of Paul's life was to organize a world-wide collection for poor Jews in Jerusalem and thus try to give his own people a striking indication that the prophecies calling for the unity of Jew and Gentile were indeed being fulfilled.

In his own personal life, there is no evidence that Paul ever abandoned the traditional practices and religious observances of the Torah except when he was living with Gentiles and saw that it would be an obstacle to the gospel.

> Although I am not bound to anyone, I made myself the slave of all so as to win over as many as possible. I became like a Jew to the Jews in order to win the Jews. To those bound by the law I became like one who is bound (although in fact I am not bound by it), that I might win those

bound by the law. To those not subject to the law
I became like one not subject to it . . . that I
might win those not subject to the law. . . . I
have made myself all things to all men in order to
save at least some of them [1 Cor. 9:20–22].

In fact, Paul made special efforts to return to Jerusalem
from time to time. When he did, he took part in the
Jewish feasts and religious observances. During his last
visit to Jerusalem, he was arrested while in the Temple
area fulfilling the sacrifices and observances that went
along with the Nazarite vow (Acts 21:26–27).

Paul and "Far-Out" Christians

I use the term "far-out" in the sense of Christians who
would be quite different in lifestyle and practices from
the ordinary Christians whom we know today. In the
early church there was a remarkable diversity among
Christians that some would find somewhat hard to accept. One group might be called the "Judeo-Christians."
These were Christians who faithfully kept all the traditional Jewish practices and observances found in the
Bible and in the oral teachings of Judaism at the time. A
number of these were converts from the Pharisees (Acts
15:5) who brought with them a most fervent and exact
observance of every detail of the Torah, as well as the
priestly codes found in the Bible and in tradition. They
looked upon Christ as the fulfilment of the Torah in every
way, especially that of love. The earliest Christians were
mostly Judeo-Christians who continued to frequent the
Temple and synagogues. They were hardly distinguished from their fellow Jews except for their own secret
home gatherings and their belief in Jesus as the chosen
Jewish Messiah (Acts 2:46–3:1).

Due to travel and business, Paul came in contact with
these Jewish Christians wherever he went. In addition to
them, there were also some Gentile Christians who took

upon themselves all the Jewish observances and practices beginning with circumcision. At no time does Paul ever tell them that they must give up their traditional Jewish observances. Also, while with them, or with non-Christian Jews, he himself kept all the details of the Torah according to his principle: "I became like a Jew to the Jews in order to win the Jews" (1 Cor. 9:20). It was only when some Jewish Christians took a determined stand that Gentile converts *must* be circumcised and keep all the Jewish laws that Paul vigorously opposed what they said (Acts 15:1–2). He even had a direct confrontation with Peter himself when the latter segregated himself from Gentile Christians on the occasion of a visit to Antioch (Gal. 2:11–14). Paul felt that the behavior of Peter and the attitude of the "Judaizers" (those who insisted on the law for Gentiles) were undermining the absolute sufficiency of faith in Jesus for salvation.

A second group of "far-out" Christians might be called the "radical enthusiasts" in Thessalonica. Some of them were saying "the day of the Lord is here" (2 Thess. 2:2). In other words, they thought that history had just about come to an end. As a result, some of them were quitting their jobs and no longer working, supporting themselves by alms. This is indicated by Paul's strong admonitions that they should work with their hands (1 Thess. 4:11; 2 Thess. 3:10). The "over-enthusiasts" believed that the Spirit was within them, instructing them about the imminent end of the world. They put great stock in prophetic utterances about the future (2 Thess. 2:2). Some of the Thessalonian Christians seemed very much influenced by the Hellenistic ideal of a religious charismatic as a spirit-filled person embued with divine strength and power. As a result they concerned themselves as little as possible with earthly matters. The all important matter was their ability to commune with the inner divine Spirit and manifest this through various psychic gifts, such as healings, exorcisms, and miracles.

The approach of Paul is not to severely condemn them

or ask that they be excommunicated as not being real Christians. Paul understands them and gently corrects them. He does not say that there should not be Christian prophetism, but he does state that there should be careful "discretion of spirits" by the community (1 Thess. 5:21). The independence of this overly charismatic group led them to criticize Paul. Paul responded merely by establishing the truth about his relations to them. His coming and preaching was indeed in power, but it was beyond that of the Thessalonian "pneumatics." It was power to transform people's lives through the gospel of God (1 Thess. 1:5–6). Paul recognizes and appreciates Christian diversity; he wishes only to correct evident abuses.

At Corinth, there were Christians so excited about the gifts of the Spirit that they longed for and preferred the more individual and emotionally felt gifts such as that of tongues. This was a prayerful ecstatic address to God in words unintelligible to the ordinary person. Because so many wished to speak in tongues, there was often disorder and confusion in the community meetings (1 Cor. 12:22). Once again, Paul does not condemn these Christians. They have a beautiful, special gift that is a witness to the presence of the Spirit. However, he carefully shows that other gifts of the Spirit that contribute better to the community should be preferred (1 Cor. 14). In addition, those so gifted should place a voluntary limitation on themselves so that the community meetings will be orderly with all having the opportunity to express themselves without confusion (1 Cor. 14:26–33). After all, "God is a God, not of confusion, but of peace" (1 Cor. 14:33).

Most significant of all, there were at Corinth and other communities Paul founded Christians who might best be called "gnostic-oriented." The word "gnosis" means nothing more than "knowledge." This knowledge centers on the conviction that all people (or at least some) have a piece of the divine, the *pneuma*, locked within them. This is unrecognized by the world which is ignorant of its true inner self. Thus people need to be awakened to know who they truly are and be able to tap this powerful presence within them. This only can come about through a special inner illuminaton or "gnosis." For these Christians, Christ would be a type of wisdom teacher who has come to this world as a representative of the true light to teach all people to find within themselves the same light and divine life that he had in himself.

Some of the difficulties Paul faces at Corinth can possibly be understood in view of the inclination of some Christians to have a gnostic-influenced view of themselves and the world. For example, Paul must place great emphasis on the resurrection of the body in 1 Corinthians 15, where he writes, "How is it that some of you say there is no resurrection of the dead!" An outright denial of the resurrection by the Corinthians would seem rather strange, for this was the central point of Paul's preaching. However, in view of gnostic depreciation of the body, the statement becomes understandable. Gnostic Christians would certainly de-emphasize the resurrection of a corruptible human body which they regarded as a prison of the divine spark within. They would prize the *present* attainment of immortality through gnosis, rather than the future expectation of an immortal body. Such a person would challenge Paul, asking, "How are the dead to be raised up? What kind of body will they have?" (1 Cor. 15:35). The gnostic de-emphasis of the flesh may explain why Paul has to place such continual and heavy emphasis on the cross and death of Jesus as opposed to the "wisdom" of his opponents (1 Cor. 2:2–3:23). It would also help understand why some Christians of rather rigid ascetical views wished to have nothing to do with sex, even in marriage (1 Cor. 1:1–40). The gnostics considered marriage to belong to the realm of the flesh, and hence as a hindrance to the Spirit.

While Paul disagrees with some of the views of gnostic-oriented Christians, he always respects them and treats them as fellow Christians. He does not condemn them or hint that they are not really Christians. On the contrary, he seems to have been open to a diversity among Christians, although he was careful not to let it go far enough to become a point of division. In doing so he was actually creating a bridge between East and West, for gnosticism appears to have had its roots in the East.

To sum up: Paul had a remarkable broadness of vision and understanding of the working of the Spirit of God in all humankind. He was able to attract non-Jews by his deep appreciation of the inner oneness in the human family placed there by the Spirit of God. His own upbringing in Judaism made it possible for him to be an agent for bringing together both Gentile and Jew in spiritual fellowship. Within the Christian community he was careful to encourage diversity without letting it go to the limits of division.

Reflections for Modern Christians

"With God there is no favoritism" (Rom. 2:11). Paul took this very seriously and saw the Spirit of God working in non-Christians, Jews, and Christians of wide diversity in lifestyle and practices. Paul did not see anyone, no matter of what race or religion, as needing something from the outside to be saved or complete. God was working in the whole universe and manifesting himself through all creation to everyone. The non-Christian religions also have their way to God, given to them by the Spirit. At the same time Paul looked realistically at the world around him and saw that belief in the risen Christ could be a new and deeper source of growth and activity for every person. He experienced this so much himself that he felt impelled to share it with others. It opened up new possibilities for the world.

From this point of view, a relationship with people of other religions or of no declared religion must be a dialog, rather than one-way traffic. If it is done from a hidden

superior attitude that you have much to give to a person
with very little, it is making a judgment on that person
that is contrary to Jesus' own directions in the Sermon on
the Mount when he said, "If you want to avoid judgment, stop passing judgment" (Matt. 7:1). Only God
himself can know and measure the work that he is doing
in a hidden way in each person. The sharing of one's faith
with another proceeds from a burning desire to communicate to others what startling changes Christ has
made in your own life. It does not come from a conde-
scending and paternal desire to help someone else who
you feel has very little. When you need that person as a
brother or sister in Christ, then you are talking with them
at the level of equality.

God's work in the world may be compared to that of a
great artist with a workroom filled with countless mas-
terpieces. The divine artist completes some pictures in a
day, some in years, some in dozens of years. But each
picture is *perfect*, because it is at the stage he wants it to be
at this time. Each painting manifests some part or quality
of the divine artist in a unique way not possessed by any
other. Hence there can be no comparison or judgments.
When all the works of art are put together, they form a
complete reflection of the great Author. Each work needs
each other one as a necessary means to know the Creator,
and to know itself as well. Whenever a very special light
does shine on one of the paintings, it is only that it may be
shared with others to put together a full image of the
Master. Such in sum must be our attitude in sharing our
faith with others.

Paul would have been saddened and shocked if he saw
Christianity today with its hundreds of denominations,
most of which are not in communion with one another.
In fact there is still open opposition between many
groups. He would see lack of oneness and intercommu-
nion as the evil involved, not the remarkable diversity
between them. He would see the latter as the work of the
Holy Spirit creating a beautiful complete image of God

reflected in human beings from many directions. Unity will come not by insisting upon it, but by encouraging, respecting, and loving this diversity as a mark of the Holy Spirit of God. Once this happens, oneness and communion will come about easily and naturally in the form that is best for all.

Within churches and denominations, many people have been alarmed at the apparent splintering into small and very diverse groups. There are many independent movements, e.g., prayer or meditation groups that carry on by themselves, "floating parishes," free ministries, and other groups that do not appear concerned that the mother churches frown on their separation, or even disregard them. At this point, we can refer to the insights of our Chapter 5. Once the church recovers its gift of the apostle, it will see these small "splinter groups" not as harmful splinters, but as a remarkable means to reach more and more people in many diverse ways. The apostolic mother church would even cooperate in starting such groups, knowing that a recognition and encouragement of diversity is the best way to approach people who come from many, many different points in their lives. By encouraging, helping to coordinate, and serving these small groups the mother church will become a real mother through taking on the role of Christ himself as a humble servant of love. The mother churches will thus reject the temptation of power and control just as Jesus did in his forty-day temptation and encounter with Satan in the desert.

13

Leadership Development

Discipleship and Leadership

For Paul the expressions "disciple of Christ" and
"Christian leader" meant the same thing. We never read
in his epistles that he regarded anyone as a "disciple of
Paul." In fact, in the whole New Testament, with the
exception of John the Baptist, the term "disciple" is used
only in reference to Christ. This is because Christians are
people who are freed from dependence on any human
teacher or master; they are dependent only on Christ, of
whom they are more partners, friends, and co-workers
than subordinates. We can understand why Paul was so
greatly disturbed when he heard news from Corinth that
the community had broken into cliques, each claiming a
special connection to some human teacher:

> As long as there are jealousy and quarrels among
> you, are you not of the flesh? And is not your
> behavior that of ordinary men? When someone
> says, "I belong to Paul" but someone else, "I
> belong to Apollos," is it not clear that you are still
> at the human level? [1 Cor. 3:3–4].

Because of this tendency to human discipleship, Paul
had to stress the part that he, Apollos, and other teachers
played. They were only servants and instruments of God
whose task it was to make people dependent on and
belong to God alone. The disciples were God's building,
God's tillage, God's temple:

After all, who is Apollos? And who is Paul? Simply ministers through whom you became believers, each of them doing only what the Lord assigned him. I planted the seed and Apollos watered it, but God made it grow. . . . We are God's co-workers, you are his cultivation, his building" [1 Cor. 3:5–9].

Paul then felt that his work was to "make himself useless" through the development of strong disciples of Christ, Christian leaders who could stand on their own two feet without looking to others for support other than that of communal help.

Trust in Individual Gifts of the Holy Spirit to Build the Community

For the Apostle Paul, "election" as a Christian was not just a personal privilege. It was rather the gift of a special mission and responsibility to the community and to the world. It meant that the Holy Spirit could now work in a new individual in a unique way for the benefit of all. There could be no "unemployment" in a Christian community. When Paul said, "I believe in the Holy Spirit," he did not mean *my* Holy Spirit, but a Spirit that was shared by all and worked in all for the benefit of all. There could be no monopoly of gifts of the Holy Spirit by any individual. Paul had his gift, that of an apostle. He trusted that others had their gifts also and refused to presume that all gifts could be concentrated in himself. He could truly say, "*I*" believe, for the act of faith was personal to him. But he would have to refer to the Spirit as *our* Spirit, for the Spirit worked in each one in a unique manner.

For Paul, the best way to develop leaders was to encourage each person to use his gift of the Holy Spirit to the fullest possible extent in order to build the community. There are three places where Paul deals specifically with this matter: 1 Cor. 12–14; Rom. 12:3–8; Eph. 4:1–16.

1 Corinthians 12–14: Paul's general principle was to encourage all gifts of the Spirit: "Do not stifle the Spirit. Do not despise prophecies . . ." (1 Thess. 5:20). Yet at Corinth some church members prided themselves on some of the flashier types of gifts, such as the gift of tongues. These gifts, while helpful to the whole community, were by nature more an individual or personal matter. In their zeal for practicing these gifts, it often happened that other members whose gifts were more directly concerned with helping others were not given enough opportunity to exercise them. This situation was the occasion of a special instruction of Paul regarding the nature and use of spiritual gifts.

Paul had to stress that the one Spirit in the community was the source of all these gifts:

> Now there are different gifts, but the same Spirit;
> there are different ministries, but the same Lord;
> there are different works, but the same God,
> who accomplishes all of them in everyone [1 Cor. 12:4–6].

Since the Spirit was one, the working of this Spirit must be for the advantage of all and never should be a hindrance to anyone:

> To each person, the manifestation of the Spirit is given for the common good [1 Cor. 12:7].

It was however God's will that there be a diversity of gifts in the community: "but it is one and the same Spirit who produces all these gifts, distributing them to each as he wills" (1 Cor. 12:11).

What was the purpose of such a diversity of gifts? First of all that there be unity in the community, that the members, being interdependent would experience their need for one another. No members could say that they were independent and that they did not need the others' gifts. Paul compares the oneness of those sharing the Holy Spirit to the unity that exists in a human body. No one member of a human body, whether head, arm, or eye can say that it is independent and does not need the others.

> There are indeed many different members, but one body. The eye cannot say to the hand, "I do not need you," any more than the head can say to the feet, "I do not need you" [1 Cor. 12:21].

Such a division of members and function was willed by God so that all the members might work together, have a real concern for each other, and share their joys and sufferings together.

> But God has so constructed the body as to give greater honor to the lowly members, that there may be no dissension in the body, but that the members may be concerned for one another. If one member suffers anything, all the members suffer with it; if one member is honored, all the members share its joy [1 Cor. 12:24–26].

Paul then applies this to the community, the body of Christ formed by people sharing his spirit: "You then are the body of Christ. Every one of you is a member of it" (1 Cor. 12:27). There are various members in this body, each with a special role to play in its growth and function: apostles, prophets, teachers, administrators, those with the gift of healing the sick, those who are for the poor, finally those with the gift of tongues (1 Cor. 12:28–31).

Paul felt that the basic matter was not so much which member you were, or what gift you had, but the underlying spirit of identification with Christ, which he called *agape*. He never defines this exactly, but according to his description in Chapter 13, it consists of the complete selflessness and deep concern for others that marked Christ himself.

As for the external expression of this inner quality in the gifts of the members, the important question was how the particular gift helped to build others in the community. In Chapter 14 alone he uses the noun "up-building" or the verb "build" seven times. This is the criterion of every spiritual gift: How much does it help to build others, to build up the community? For this reason he gives a primacy to prophecy, which is by nature dedicated to helping others, and puts at the bottom of the list the gift of tongues, which is primarily self-edifying:

> Seek eagerly after love. Set your hearts on spir-
> itual gifts—above all, the gift of prophecy. A
> man who speaks in a tongue is talking not to men
> but to God. No one understands him because he
> utters mysteries in the Spirit. The prophet on the
> other hand speaks to men for their upbuilding,
> their encouragement and their consolation. He
> who speaks in a tongue builds up himself, but he
> who prophesies builds up the Church [1 Cor.
> 14:1–4].

From 1 Corinthians then, we can see the great importance that Paul attaches to the development of the gifts God has given to each Christian. Paul had one gift, that of an apostle. But for the function and growth of the body of Christ, others had a necessary role and responsibility. A profound trust in the gifts of others was essential for Paul. The whole community was informed with one Spirit and depended on the contribution of each person. Through each person, the one Spirit acted in a special and unique manner for the benefit of all. Paul's way of developing leaders was through the recognition, trust, and encouragement of the special gift and role of each member of the community.

Romans 12:3–8: In Romans 12:3–8, Paul presents essentially the same picture as in Corinthians: the use of every gift of the Holy Spirit to build the body of Christ. What he does add is a stress on the full development of these gifts and their intense application in the service of others.

Evidently there were some in the community who prided themselves in the special gifts that they had. Paul warns them that the basis of comparison is not in the gift itself but in the "proportion of faith" that God has given. This "proportion of faith" is measured by the extent that a person uses a particular gift to serve and build the community. For faith means adhesion to God himself, and this faith manifests itself or works through *agape,* a real concern for the needs and growth of others (cf. Gal. 5:6).

> I warn each of you not to think more highly of himself than he ought. Let him estimate himself soberly, in keeping with the measure of faith God has apportioned him. Just as each of us has one body with many members, and not all the members have the same function, so too we, though many, are one body in Christ, and individually members one of another. We have gifts that differ according to the favor bestowed on each of us [Rom. 12:3–6].

The gifts are not to be a source of pride resulting from comparison, but they are to be whole-heartedly applied for the service of the community. They are also to be fully developed and practiced with that complete human involvement that characterizes the perfect gift of self:

> It may be the gift of ministry; it should be used for service. One who is a teacher should use his gift for teaching. One with the power of exhortation should exhort. He who gives alms should do so generously; he who rules should exercise his

authority with care; he who performs acts of mercy should do so cheerfully [Rom. 12:7–8].

The Roman axiom *age quod agis*, "Really do what you are doing," would apply here. Father Barnabas Ahern, C.P., commenting on the passage, has a beautiful paragraph describing this intense devotion of one's personal gifts to the service of the community:

> The inspired preacher, for instance, should speak only according to the measure of his God-given message; one with the gift of serving the community should direct it to the needs of the community; the gifted catechist should devote himself to teaching; the inspired counsellor should busy himself in giving advice and encouragement. If one has alms to give, his task is to bestow these without seeking ulterior aims. Those in charge of good works should watch over them with care. Those engaged in works of mercy should radiate joy [*New Testament Reading Guide* (Collegeville, Minn.: Liturgical Press)].

Ephesians 4:1–16: In this passage, the author looks at the body of Christ from a different perspective. Here the risen Christ himself is described as the head of not just one community but of the whole church. It is he, ascended into heaven, who distributes his gifts to the church. The purpose of the various gifts is to promote the progress and advancement of the whole organism so that it becomes more and more like Christ himself:

> It is he who gave apostles, prophets, evangelists, pastors and teachers in roles of service for the faithful to build up the body of Christ, till we become one in faith and in the knowledge of God's Son and form that perfect man who is Christ come to full stature [Eph. 4:11–13].

We may conclude then that Paul was able to so effectively encourage local leadership because of his willingness to see a special place for the personal gifts of each person in the work of building up the community. He had a deep trust in the Holy Spirit working in each person in a unique way. As a result he was able to concentrate on his special calling, that of establishing new foundations. He was able to go from place to place confident that the Holy Spirit would work in each community in all its members, provided they were given the responsibility and opportunity to use their personal gifts for the service of all. For Paul, becoming a Christian was not a passive privilege but the sharing of a new responsibility—the sharing of Christ's own mission to build a community of men and women.

Reflections for Modern Christians

The crying need in the world today is for real leaders—men and women who will not stand by passively in the face of the evident injustices, inequality, and corruption that we see in government and society today. Effective change can be brought about only by courageous people who live according to the principles they believe in and do not hesitate to infuse them into the world around us.

Yet leaders such as these need to be trained and formed. The ideal place should be in the Christian community. Yet many communities seem to have an atmosphere of inert passivism where people still look up to others for leadership and are dependent on a small group within the church who appear to have concentrated all the gifts and talents of the Holy Spirit within themselves. If this happens, it will be hardly the place where active and courageous young leaders will be developed for their God-given mission of transforming the modern world.

Paul's conviction that there should be no human discipleship in the church should be taken seriously. It was not only his view but a strong New Testament position. The Gospel of Matthew strongly emphasizes this in the words of Jesus, "Avoid being called teachers. Only one is your teacher, the Messiah" (Matt. 23:10). During his earthly career, the mission and powers of the Twelve are exactly those of Jesus (Matt. 9:35–10:1)—they could heal the sick, perform exorcisms, and preach the good news of the kingdom. However, they are not to make disciples of themselves. Only after the resurrection are they told "go, make disciples of all nations." This is because they will be making disciples of the risen Jesus, not themselves, by baptizing, by plunging others into the Father, Son, and Holy Spirit (Matt. 28:19). The Johannine tradition confirms this view. Jesus told the crowds after the multiplication of the loaves that the Scriptures would be fulfilled which said, "They shall all be taught by God"—for everyone who has listened to God will come to him (John 6:45). The author of the first Letter of John warns against trusting exclusively in human teachers, since the Holy Spirit alone is the real Teacher: "This means you have no need for anyone to teach you. Rather, . . . his anointing teaches you about all things" (1 John 2:27).

With this in view, it is easy to see that whatever gift of the Spirit you have is meant to be shared with others. *Agape*, or love, means building up others as well as ourselves. When there is this beautiful and loving sharing of the gifts of the Spirit in a community, then all people can become effective leaders and teachers in the world around them. They will be teachers in the full sense of the word—those whose lifestyle is so modeled on that of Christ that others can see a visible image of the path and values they should follow·in life.

14

Community Witness

A Community Goal

To know what a community witness for Christ meant
in a Pauline church, we must first know what goal each
community looked forward to. From the epistles we see
that the "omega" point of a Christian community was a
final community of children of God resurrected through
and with the Spirit of Christ their brother. Paul described
his own call very simply: that God had revealed his Son
in him (Gal. 1:16). By this he meant that God had chosen
to share the Spirit of his Son with him, so he could know
what it meant to be able to deal with God as his own
father through union with Jesus: "The proof that you are
sons is in the fact that God has sent forth into our hearts
the spirit of his Son which cries out 'Abba' ('Father!')"
(Gal. 4:6).

Yet this spirit of sonship had only effected a beginning;
its full revelation and unfolding in himself and others
was something yet to come:

> Not only that, but we ourselves, although we
> have the Spirit as first fruits, groan inwardly
> while we await the redemption of our bodies. In
> hope we were saved [Rom. 8:23–24].

So Paul saw the final goal of himself and others as a risen community of children of God at the resurrection, brothers and sisters of Christ and of one another through the sharing of the Spirit of the Son of God.

This "forward look" to the fellowship of the Son of God at the resurrection became basic to the belief of every community that Paul helped to initiate. Since it was so familiar to them, he could write to the Thessalonians: "Who after all, if not you, will be our hope or joy, or the crown we exult in, before our Lord Jesus Christ at his coming? You are our boast and our delight" (1 Thess. 2:19).

The same expectation appears in every major epistle. We may note 2 Cor. 4:14: "We believe and so we speak, knowing that he who raised up the Lord Jesus will raise us up also along with Jesus, and will place both us and you in his presence." Also Romans 8:11:

> But if the Spirit of him who raised Jesus from the dead dwells in you, then he who raised Christ from the dead will bring your mortal bodies to life also through his Spirit dwelling in you.

A Covenant Brotherhood

With a community in heaven as a goal, it is easy to see that the community on earth must be a reflection and preparation for it. This is not just in the sense of preparing for the future, but in actively realizing the community of brotherhood made possible by the real present possession of the Spirit as a pledge and initiator of what is to come.

In the epistles to the Thessalonians the expression "brother" or "brothers" is used twenty-eight times; in all the epistles over 120 times. It was the common term used to designate a fellow Christian. Yet it was more than just a designation; it reflected the deep responsibility and concern for one another that was characteristic of those who shared the Spirit of Christ.

This concern would especially be manifested in face of the real needs of others. At the time of the death of relatives or close friends of the community Christians would show their brotherly concern by comforting their bereaved friends through their mutual hope in the resurrection. Paul's teaching on the resurrection of the dead in 1 Thess. 4:13–18 is given with the express purpose that this might be a source of hope for those in deep sorrow. And so he adds the injunction, "Console one another with this message" (1 Thess. 4:18).

In case any brother should go astray through human weakness, he should always be confident that his brothers would seek after him to bring him back:

> My brothers, if someone is detected in sin, you who live by the Spirit should gently set him right, each of you trying to avoid falling into temptation himself. Help carry one another's burdens; in that way you will fulfill the law of Christ [Gal. 6:1–2].

This "law of Christ" is based on the directive of the Master to seek out and help a brother who has sinned (Matt. 18:15–18). Then once the brother has been found, he must be offered the same generous forgiveness that the members of the community have experienced from their union with Christ:

> In place of this, be kind to one another, compassionate, and mutually forgiving, just as God has forgiven you in Christ [Eph. 4:32].

This spirit of brotherly help especially manifested itself at the community meeting. Paul was deeply conscious that the Master had promised to send a *Paraclete*, meaning a defender, helper, one who stands by and encourages. Since this *Paraclete* dwelt in people of faith, he would show himself through the members of the community as they strove to help and encourage one another in view of their common faith. For this reason, Paul considered the gift of prophecy among the greatest of spiritual gifts. For it was this gift that was especially directed to inspiring, exhorting, and encouraging others. "The prophet, on the other hand, speaks to men for their upbuilding, their encouragement, their consolation" (1 Cor. 14:3).

In fact, Paul thought that there should be such truth and sincerity present in community meetings that unbelievers who entered would find this spirit contagious; that seeing the honesty with which the members faced one another and God through their faith, they themselves would be almost "forced" to take an honest account of themselves:

> But if an unbeliever or an uninitiate enters while all are uttering prophecy, he will be taken to task by all and called to account by all, and the secrets of his heart will be laid bare. Falling prostrate, he will worship God, crying out, "God is truly among you" [1 Cor. 14:24–25].

For unbelievers then, the brotherly spirit of mutual help in the community would be the most convincing argument. They would be joining a community in which the Spirit of Jesus made possible such mutual help and encouragement.

A Positive Morality

By a positive morality, we do not mean just positive principles of conduct. Paul usually presumes that his Christians know what is ethically correct. Many of his ethical instructions are almost literally the same as pagan admonitions of his time. What he has in mind is a new basis of morality: the presence of a sanctifying Spirit of Jesus that claims them as his own and thus gives them the responsibility to live in a manner corresponding to their being temples of God.

Thus Paul warns the Thessalonians that those who give themselves to immorality have rejected God and the spirit of holiness to which they have been called:

> God has not called us to immorality, but to holiness. Hence, he who rejects these instructions rejects, not man but God, who sends his Holy Spirit upon you [1 Thess. 4:7–8].

Paul writes even more strongly to the Corinthians, telling them that their bodies belong to the Lord as members of Christ; hence they must never give their bodies to another in fornication.

> Do you not see that your bodies are members of Christ? Would you have me take Christ's members and make them members of a prostitute? God forbid! [1 Cor. 6:15].

In their relations to one another, it is likewise their mutual sharing of the same sanctifying Spirit that is the motivating force behind good conduct, rather than precepts alone: "See to it, then, that you put an end to lying; let everyone speak the truth to his neighbor, for we are members of one another" (Eph. 4:25).

Those who had been given to stealing, taking away what belonged to their neighbors, should give themselves over to hard work so they might have something they could share with the poor:

> The man who has been stealing must steal no

> longer; rather let him work with his hands at
> honest labor so that he will have something to
> share with those in need [Eph. 4:28].

Those who had been prone to careless speech should now consider how their words can be a source of help to others: "Never let evil talk pass your lips; say only the good things men need to hear, things that will really help them" (Eph. 4:29).

Community Witness to the World

Is the Christian community to stand out in the world as only a great receptacle of God's favor, or do they have the role, as members of Christ, to be his channel of grace to the whole world? Paul answers this, writing to the Philippians:

> In everything you do, act without grumbling
> or arguing; prove yourselves innocent and
> straightforward, beyond reproach in the midst of
> a twisted and depraved generation—among
> whom you shine like the stars in the sky while
> holding fast the word of life [Phil. 2:14–16].

Here we see that the community, as children of God, should be a shining light to the world. The kinship of the children of God would be so manifest that it would be an inspiration to the world, and, in addition, prompt others to join the community.

Here Paul refers to one part of the Christian witness, yet he does not limit it to this. He always emphasized that Christ's resurrection was over every power in the world. The complete victory would be only through Christians; it would be accomplished not by withdrawing from the world, but by bringing Christ's power to bear in every human activity. We do not have any master plan for this in the epistles. We do, however, see some evidence to point out that Christians are to be a leaven in the world; their ideal is not separation but transformation. Yet they are to accomplish this not by force but by love. They will not seek to impose from without but to transform from within.

In regard to government and civic duties, certainly Christians would know more than others how much they could suffer in persecution because of government officials. Yet Paul was concerned to point out that authority, when used properly for the good of all, was an instrument of God and that the Christians' attitude should be one of respect and obedience:

> You pay taxes for the same reason, magistrates being God's ministers who devote themselves to his service with unremitting care. Pay to each one his due; taxes to whom taxes are due; toll to whom toll is due; respect and honor to everyone who deserves them [Rom. 13:7].

This respect and obedience, as well as attention to civic duties, would be the way to bring Christ's power and influence into the heart of government.

In regard to a person's state in life, occupation, or employment, becoming a Christian did not mean finding a new situation in life. It meant rather to make the best of, and even transform the situation in which one was found. Even slaves, despite their apparently hopeless situation, should not feel that they could not be good Christians and thus be transforming influences on both their fellow slaves and their masters:

> Everyone ought to continue as he was when he was called. Were you a slave when your call came? Give it no thought. Even supposing you could go free, you would be better off making the most of your slavery. The slave called in the Lord is a freedman of the Lord, just as the freedman

who has been called is a slave of Christ [1 Cor. 7:21–22].

Likewise if a man becomes a Christian while his wife remains an unbeliever, his first thought should not be how he can separate from her and escape a possibly difficult situation, but rather how he can sanctify her by his good example:

> If any brother has a wife who is an unbeliever but is willing to live with him, he must not divorce her. And if any woman has a husband who is an unbeliever but is willing to live with her, she must not divorce him. The unbelieving husband is consecrated by his believing wife; the unbelieving wife is consecrated by her believing husband [1 Cor. 7:12–14].

Paul does not spell out how the Christian can penetrate every sphere of human life. He does however say, "Brothers, each of you should continue before God in the condition of life that was his when he was called" (1 Cor. 7:24). In other words, the call to be a Christian does not mean withdrawal, separation, or change, but rather a greater commitment to the vocation in life to which one has dedicated oneself. In this way, Paul developed the beginnings of a theology of the Christian lay person. He saw that the Christians' most powerful witness could be indirect. They could perform the same work or occupation as non-Christians, whether as a husband or wife, father or mother, whether in the community or in work, but now their work would be singled out by their dedication and ideal of excellence inspired by the love of Christ.

Paul had a new expression to sum up his ideal of Christian life in the world. He called it "in the Lord." It was his special insight into a unique way of transforming the ordinary actions of each day, or of any person in any state or occupation of life. It did not matter whether it was a parent or child, a husband, wife, slave, freedman, or lord. "In the Lord" meant that people were so transfigured and transformed by the Spirit of God that they were shining, radiant, and luminous vessels of God's presence and love in the world. Paul expressed this in the following words: "God, who said, 'Let light shine out of darkness,' has shone in our hearts, that we in turn might make known the glory of God shining on the face of Christ" (2 Cor. 4:6). With this view of their new identity in Christ and the transforming presence of the Spirit, it no longer mattered who a person was, or what he or she did in the world. Each was a vessel and mirror of God's own love in the world. The only important matter was the ideal of Christ himself, that of a humble loving servant of God who would simply allow the light and love of the Spirit to shine and manifest itself in every action of the day.

"In the Lord" meant a new degree of intensity and excellence in every action because it became just one more opportunity and outlet for heartfelt love shown by humble service to the needs of others. As a result, Paul could say, "Whatever you do, work at it with your whole being. Do it for the Lord rather than for men" (Col. 3:23). This ideal will mean that Christians will dedicate themselves wholeheartedly to whatever work or profession they find. Real Christians will be distinguished by a dedicated excellence in all professions and walks of life, whether it be care of lawns, service of people, teaching, or technology.

Finally, Paul was no doubt asked what the Christian attitude should be in the face of hostility and even persecution on the part of the world. The natural tendency would be to reply in kind, or at most to bear patiently and leave retribution to God. The latter was the attitude of the Qumran community. Paul went much further than this. He wrote to the Romans:

> Bless your persecutors; bless and do not curse them. . . . Never repay injury with injury. See

that your conduct is honorable in the eyes of all.
If possible, live peaceably with everyone. Beloved, do not avenge yourselves, leave that to
God's wrath, for it is written, "Vengeance is
mine; I will repay," says the Lord. But "If your
enemy is hungry, feed him; if he is thirsty, give
him something to drink; for by doing this you
will heap burning coals upon his head." Be not
conquered by evil, but conquer evil with good
[Rom. 12:14–21].

The Christian way of changing the world in face of
opposition is not through force but by love. It is through
the principle of nonviolence, correctly understood. It is
nonviolence that is not merely passive nonresistance, but
an active program of trying to win others over by positive
concern and loving action.

To sum up: The community witness for Christ in a
Pauline church consisted of the following: (1) The security of a definite community goal in Christ, to which
people could devote all their energies. (2) A covenant
brotherhood expressed both in worship and mutual
help. The greatest difficulties and struggles of life could
be faced with the help of brothers and sisters in whom
the Spirit of Christ was truly a *Paraclete,* an encouraging
and supporting advocate. Here a new morality—not
based on precepts but on deep reverence and service of
one another—was the great motivation for holiness.
(3) The opportunity of making a real impression on the
world, not by withdrawing from it but by greater engagement in it through a complete dedication of oneself
to work in the world.

Application for Modern Christians

There is no argument in the eyes of the world as powerful as that of a community moving toward true
brotherhood and unity. In John 17:21 we have the prayer

of Jesus, "that all may be one . . . , that the world may believe that you sent me." Thomas Aquinas, commenting on this verse, notes that nothing demonstrates the truth of the Christian faith more than the unity and love that exists between Christians.

This fraternal union can exist only where there is true dialog between members of the community. In the time of Paul, the service of the Word was an important occasion for this. After the reading of the Scriptures in the community, the members strove to examine themselves seriously before the Word; then once they had seen themselves honestly, they encouraged one another to strengthen their commitment to Christ and one another. For them, the *Paraclete* was truly a Spirit who spoke through people to help and encourage them.

Modern apostles then will do all that they can to help promote a spirit of real dialog among Christians themselves. They would do well to follow the lead of Paul: to bring people together in small groups for a similar service of the Word. This can start with a reading from the Scriptures by one of them; following this, there can be a silent time for reflection. This can continue for as long as the group wishes. After this, those who wish may share their personal response to the Word of God with the others in view of helping, and then in turn being helped by others. This should all be done with complete freedom and openness, each one being free to be silent or to speak. The sharing can be followed by a period of prayer for the pressing concerns of the group.

Today especially the world is searching for meaningful motivation for leading a good moral life. Laws alone do not suffice. The idea of offending God must be completed by sufficient understanding of the *horizontal* implications of sin. A stronger emphasis on the motivations that flow from a deep reverence and respect of a member of a covenant brotherhood will do much to encourage a world that knows what is right but has not the strength and motivation to accomplish it.

Paul continually emphasized to his communities that becoming a Christian did not mean withdrawal from the world but on the contrary a greater engagement within the world. Likewise, people of the world today should feel that in becoming a Christian they do not abandon in the least their commitment to the world, but rather increase it without measure "in the Lord," due to the new strength they have in Christ and their brothers and sisters.

As a final comment, the Christian ideal has often been embodied in the past in the Christian commune, where there has been a complete sharing of life together, economically, spiritually, and socially. The religious orders and the monastic life were usually the only place where this was done. As a result, the participants were celibate, with men and women living apart from one another in their own communities. The time has come for a real restoration of the ideal of the Christian commune— this time no longer limited to celibates or religious communities but extended and shared by married people and children as well. The Christian commune can thus be a place for dedicated apostles, men and women who wish to be at the service of Christian communities in the world. It will also be their preferred base of operation and support as they go out to the world to fulfil the highest vocation of the apostle. This vocation, like Paul's, is to make Christ known where he is either unknown or has been forgotten.